Exploration from Lindun to Columbus

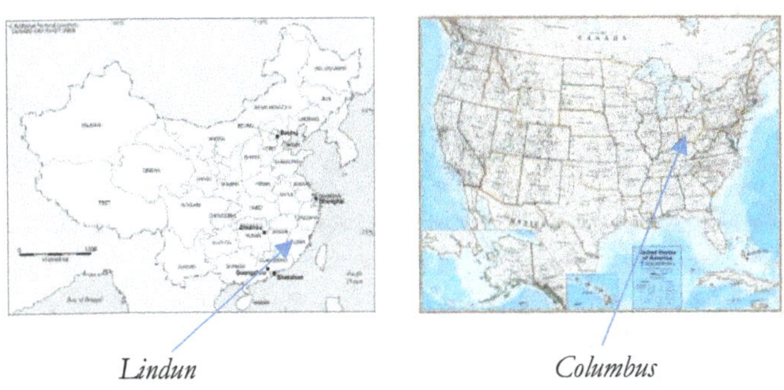

Lindun

Columbus

By
Walter Lin

Dedication

I dedicate this book to my family and those who helped me during my journey from Lindun to Columbus.

Table of Contents

Introduction

I had a long and challenging journey from Lindun, a small, rural village in southeastern China, to Columbus, Ohio, a quintessential American city in the Midwest region of the United States. It included my exploration in the following places: Lindun, Changtai (a town in Fujian province), Tsinghua University in Beijing, Shanghai Jiaotong University (SJTU), MA Institute of China in Shanghai, the University of Iowa Hawkeye in Iowa City, Florida State University Seminoles in Tallahassee, UIUC (the University of Illinois at Urbana-Champaign) Illini, EM, and SP Corporation in Kansas City Chief, YO/JC Corporation in York Pennsylvania, LE/EM/VE Corporation in Columbus Ohio Buckeye.

The initial purpose of writing this book was to let my kids, Sophia and Patrick, remember their roots. It also helped them understand how I led a challenging life after losing my father at less than three years old and how I made my way from a poor village in China to Columbus, Ohio, USA. My life stories can inspire young people to strive for a better life and career during challenging periods. This book should interest readers intrigued by the general history of how China had developed from the 1960s to the 1990s, the current status of rural China, and how a new immigrant family has experienced this new land since the 1990s. It gives parental insight into how a loving father went through many sleepless nights to find ways to pull away a struggling teenager from failure while fighting multiple diseases himself. The unique career experience described in the book will also benefit young professionals. Many extended family members, relatives, friends, alumni, colleagues, and hometown folks from every stage of my life in China and the USA will be interested in the paths I have taken throughout all these years, as described in this book.

I wrote this book with my heart and soul. It had been much more painful than expected to revisit my past, especially the painful childhood back in Lindun, those difficult journeys before 1985, and the culturally challenging and stressful life in the USA. It was like reopening an old scar that had been healed for a while. It caused much stress just thinking about surviving those difficult times and being here now. Frequently, I had to stop and rest for a few days before I could return to writing this book. Sometimes, I wanted to give up this writing project to return to a peaceful life.

I wondered if life would be easier if I chose to go to a 2-year college in 1978 and had a full-time job back in my hometown to support myself and my family in 1980. Instead, I went to an intensive 2-year high school and was admitted to Tsinghua University through a national college entrance exam at 15. According to US News, Tsinghua University is one of the best universities in the world. It has been one of the two best universities in China for many years. I also wondered what life would be like if I had chosen to stay in Shanghai in 1992 to have a relatively peaceful life instead of leaving everything I had fought for and gained behind to pursue a Ph.D. in the USA. Lastly, I wondered how life would be different if I chose to stay in the USA to live a relatively comfortable life in 2003 instead of returning to SJTU to teach as a professor for two years, leaving behind my wife and two young kids. SJTU has been considered one of the seven best universities in China.

Part I– Life in China

Chapter 1
Father's Funeral at The Eve of Chinese New Year in 1968

In my distant memory, from before I was three years old, I remember a group of people carrying a coffin climbing up a small hill near Shiheng village of Lindun on the afternoon of Chinese New Year's Eve of 1968. The coffin was slowly laid down into a pit and gradually covered with dirt. **The person in the coffin was my father, who just passed away that morning at the age of 43.** Mother and my older brothers were crying with a small group of crows cawing nearby over the trees and sky. It was raining lightly in that valley that day. I often visited this site alone or with other family members later. At that age, I was too young to understand what it meant to me and the whole family. I did not cry as other family members did. I was carried by others all the way up to the grave and back home. Mother told me later that she purchased about 0.75 kg of pork belly that afternoon after the funeral and cooked some simple meals for the whole family on Chinese New Year's Eve. **At that time, Mother was 40 years old and was left with five kids ranging from two to 19 years old.**

I was born in April 1965 when my father had been sick with Tuberculosis (TB) for three years. My father was a rural Chinese physician and pharmacist (郎中) who owned a small store that sold Chinese herbal medicine. My mother mostly stayed home, taking care of five children. I had four older brothers. The oldest brother, TJ Lin, DaGe as I called him, was 16 years older than me. The 2nd oldest brother, CJ Lin, ErGe as I called him, was 12 years older than me. The 3rd oldest brother, JJ Lin, SanGe as I called him, was six years older than me. The 4th oldest brother, XJ Lin, SiGe as I called him, was three years older than me.

Chapter 2
Lindun and Changtai

Lindun is a village in southeastern China that is about 30 km away from Xiamen airport. Xiamen is a major city in Fujian Province, which is about 2800 km away from Beijing, as shown in the following map.

Lindun is part of the Changtai District in Zhangzhou City. Zhangzhou City is part of Fujian Province. Lindun has had a population of about 10000 to 30000 for most of the last 60 years. 95% are peasants. The remaining are teachers of local schools and staff to run stores, shops, clinics, etc. Before 1975, there was a small downtown area with one small clinic, one school, several retail stores, one public cafeteria, and one small motel. The school site housed elementary, middle, and high schools at different periods. It was called Lindun Wuqi School during the Cultural Revolution period up to 1978 to honor a speech event by Chairman Mao Zedong. The motel was exclusively for the rare visitors. There was a short street of less than 100 meters through this downtown area. My family used to have a store on this street and had used it as the family home and the pharmacy store since the time of my grandfather. There are multiple smaller villages (called Dadui) in Lindun, including Shiheng, Linxi, Qiaomei, Jiandu, and Meigong. Our home belongs to Shiheng and sits in the central part of Lindun. Most of the population in Lindun had the last name Lin, except for Jiangdu village. Jiandu had the last name of Liang for the majority of its people.

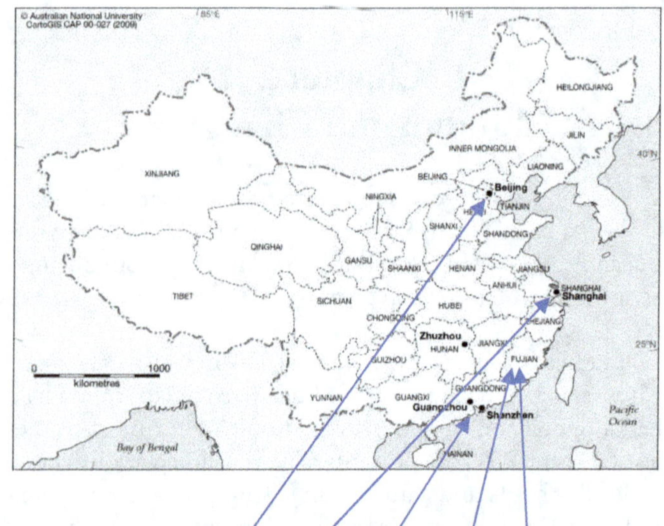

Map of China (Beijing, Shanghai, Hongkong, Lindun, Xiamen)

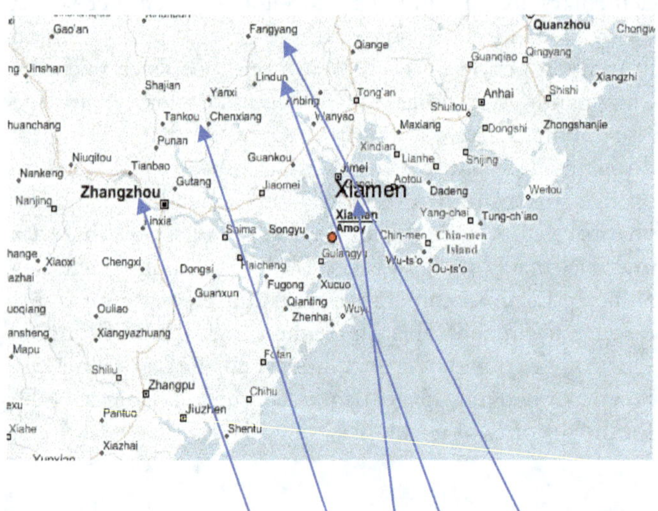

Map of South Fujian (Zhangzhou, Changtai, Xiamen, Lindun, and Fangyang)

Grave of Father   Home   Lindun Central Elementary and Middle School

Map of Lindun

Chapter 3
Parents

3.1 Father

My father, SS Lin, was a rural Chinese physician and pharmacist. He passed away from TB on the Chinese New Year's Eve of 1968 at the age of 43. I was less than three years old at that time. He might've missed good medical treatment in Xiamen before 1968 because there were violent fights between different groups of Red Guards during the Cultural Revolution. I barely had any memory of him. My father was born and grew up in Lindun. His father, my grandfather, was born in Jiandu and had the last name Liang. My grandfather came to my current family in Shiheng at a very young age. Jiandu village was about 3 km away from our current village, Shiheng. My grandmother's family had no son in Shiheng then, so their parents bought a young boy to be the future son-in-law. This was a common practice then because most families were very poor. Most people had a short life expectancy then. **From my mother, I learned that my father's father, my grandfather, passed away when my father was only 16 in 1941. My father was left with himself, a younger brother at 9, my mom at 12, and his mother (my grandmother).** My mom came to my current family when she was only eight years old as the future wife of my father. **My father inherited that small pharmacy store from my grandfather and had to run it to support the whole family at 16. My grandmother had a bound foot and could not walk long distances and work on the farm.** My father had been successful economically in this small business, and the family lived reasonably well during that period. In the 1950s, my father had to give up his small pharmacy store to join the local government-owned clinic as a pharmacist and physician in rural areas. He worked there until he died in

1968. I was told he had beautiful Chinese writing, was mostly self-taught, and had probably very limited basic education before his father died. He was skinny and smoked a lot, which might lead to his lung diseases eventually. All my neighbors told me my father was kind and helpful to others, especially poor families. He provided a lot of free service and free medicine to those who couldn't afford it. At some point in his life, my father burnt many debt receipts from families who couldn't afford to pay him back. We still found a collection of debt receipts from others after his death. I was told that SiGe and I were lucky enough to be admitted into four-year colleges after 1979, probably because my father did many nice things for the community. A Chinese God was helping us one way or another (福有福报). Father had been nice to almost everyone in the community, had a good temper, and probably never argued with anyone. The following was the only picture of my father I got from my aunt, my uncle's wife, in 2010. It was taken probably in the 1960s.

The Only Picture of My Father

3.2 Mother and Her Supernatural Farewell Before Death

Miserable Childhood

My mother, MX Huang, was a housewife and peasant. My mother's life was miserable at the beginning. She was born into a peasant family in Fangyang, a small neighboring town in Lindun. Her father was a peasant and then a beggar (乞丐) begging for food, house by house, to feed his family. Probably, he had lost the capacity to work on a farm. **My mother's father died in 1931 when my mother was only three years old. My mother's mom had to re-marry a local bandit (outlaw) with my mother to survive as one of several wives. However, she passed away too in 1936 when my mother was only eight years old. As an orphan, my mother was sold to my father's family for eight Yuan (Old Chinese Yuan) that year.** At that time, it was common for a family with boys to buy a girl at a very young age to be raised to be the future wife. My father's family did that, so my mother came to this family as a future wife of my father (童养媳妇). I heard later that my mother came to this 3rd new family at eight years old, probably had suffered a lot from her previous life, and understood how hard it was to survive. At that age, she worked very hard in this new family, getting up early daily to help her new mother, my grandmother at her father's side, cook and feed livestock, including pigs, chickens, and ducks. She also helped grow vegetables on nearby farms. It seemed this new family accepted and treated her well because she was hardworking and sensitive as a newcomer. She could then have a reasonably normal life as most other Chinese people from 1936 to 1968 before my father passed away.

Normal Youth

My father and my mother got married in 1948. Their first son, my oldest brother DaGe, was born in 1949. My mother was very busy raising six kids in the next few years. Her only daughter died at the age of 3, who would be between my 2nd oldest brother ErGe and 3rd oldest brother SanGe. She said my father could not help with any housework, and she needed to do all of it herself even when she was pregnant with small kids. My grandmother passed away sometime in the 1950s, which further burdened my mother's family load. Of course, my father had been busy with his small pharmacy store and saw patients as a rural physician to support the family. This was probably the best and most normal life my mother had in her entire life.

Hardship of Widow Life at Middle Age

On New Year's Eve of 1968, my father passed away from a six-year struggle with TB. **My mother was 40 years old at that time and started another period of miserable life with the whole family. She had five children: three years old, six years old, nine years old, 15 years old, and 19 years old.** When my father passed away, we lost the only family income. My mother had to work as a peasant on farms. DaGe graduated from a two-year teaching college and got a job soon to help support our family for a short period of time. He married an illiterate local village girl. She could not get along well with my mother. There were a lot of arguments and physical fights between them. **DaGe moved out to live his own life with his wife soon after. My mother was left alone with four kids in 1970. My 2nd oldest brother, ErGe, was forced to quit high school at 16 and worked as a peasant to support the family. Similarly, my 3rd oldest brother, SanGe, also dropped out of school at 11 when he was only in 4th grade to help support the family.** In the 1970s, peasants in my village had very low and unstable incomes, probably about 0.50 yuan per day for an adult like ErGe, working 10 hours per day. One US dollar was equivalent to eight Chinese Yuan (RMB) in the 1990s. There was only a small piece of land to farm in my village, probably less than one Mu per person.

One mu was about 0.1 acre. My mother could only earn about 0.35 yuan daily as she also needed to care for small kids like me. My 3rd oldest brother, SanGe, could only earn up to about 0.25 yuan daily as a child. At that time, one pound of pork cost about 0.70 yuan. In my memory, we never had fried eggs and fried pork because they were too expensive. We did raise chickens, ducks, and pigs at home. But they were mostly for sale to get cash in return for buying necessities like cooking oil, salt, clothes, school items, and others. What my mother tried to do was to keep all family members alive. We frequently ran out of rice from April to May each year before the harvest season and needed to borrow from relatives. We had to eat cheap vegetables and sweet potatoes to avoid going hungry, as my mother could grow some on our limited self-managed land.

We never had birthday parties for any family members. This was why I didn't know the exact birthdays of my mother and my brothers until now. It also led me to a life without the tradition of celebrating birthdays when I had my own family. I did not even know my birthday until I had to fill out some school forms. I needed to ask my brother at home to go to Shiheng village headquarters to check. My mother simply forgot the exact birthdays of her children as we did not celebrate, especially after she got older. We had a bedroom of about 16 square meters for the whole family. It could barely accommodate one big bed, one small bed, one wood box, and one cabinet for all our clothes. The king-size bed was for my mother, me, SanGe, and SiGe. The twin-size bed was for ErGe. One kitchen outside that bedroom had one dining table and several small chairs. We also had one storeroom. My father passed away in that storeroom, and we didn't sleep in that room for many years. **Frequently, my mother cried at the graveyard of my father on the mountain hill nearby because of the hardship she faced. She complained to him about why he had left a group of young children for her to raise.**

In my childhood, only one uncle, my father's brother, lived in the same neighborhood. There was another distant uncle who lived in Fangyang. This distant uncle was my mother's distant cousin when she lived with him from three to eight years old. I grew up with few relatives without grandparents or aunts due to my parents' unusual family history. **My mother later told me that some relatives chose to avoid us after my father passed away because we were too poor.** They were probably afraid that we might borrow food or money from them. A widow with a group of small children in a poor rural village in China in the 1970s had very low social status, too. One distant cousin raised partly by my grandmother (father's side) did help because he had a relatively better life than us. We could borrow rice from them every year. **The situation further deteriorated after DaGe, the only adult child, moved out with his wife to live their own life in 1970.** His wife and my mother argued and even fought physically frequently on pretty much anything, probably because we were too poor. I remember fighting with DaGe's wife physically to help defend my mother together with SiGe when I was about six to eight years old. Mother had a strong and bad temper, probably from her tough young life. She liked to lecture other family members repeatedly, which others resented.

Normal Widow Life

Life started to improve after 1976 when ErGe got a job in a furniture factory to fill in my father's left-over non-farming position. He could then have a stable monthly salary of about 18 yuan, which was much better than his income as a peasant. One yuan was about 0.125 US dollars in the 1990s, and one pound of pork cost about 0.70 Yuan in 1976. At that time, I began to see a smiling face from my mother. My family's social status improved because of ErGe's new job. ErGe was very responsible for supporting this family. He frequently brought good food home, including pork, and gave money to my mother. SanGe was

17 years old and old enough to earn cash as a peasant. In 1977, China opened to the outside world and restored the national college entrance exam after the shutdown in 1966. SiGe and I were in middle and high school then, respectively. We started to feel excited about studying to enter college. Only 2 % to 3% of high school students could attend college at that time. SiGe and I started studying hard as we knew this would be the only way to escape poverty in rural villages. In 1978, I was selected as one of about 45 gifted high school freshmen in the district through a national entrance exam for high schools and two-year colleges. I was only 13 years old and went to the central town of Changtai District (XiangCheng) to live in a dorm in the high school. This was a happy moment for the whole family, including my mother. In 1979, SiGe was accepted into a four-year college, Fujian Agriculture University, which was rare in Lindun and the 1st time in my family. In 1980, I was admitted to Tsinghua University in Beijing, the first in the district's history to be accepted through a national college entrance exam. There were only 80 students in the whole Fujian Province to be admitted to Tsinghua in 1980. Tsinghua University is one of the best universities in the world and has been one of the two best universities in China for more than 100 years. Most students would not dare to apply for this university because it was too difficult to get in. The whole district, including Lindun, knew my name, story, and family. Some unknown relatives showed up after their disappearance for a long time. My mother was quite happy during those years. However, we were still very poor because my brother and I needed money to attend college. Our economic situation improved in 1983 when SiGe graduated from college. He got a job as a teacher in a 2-year college in Jiangxi Province. It was further enhanced in 1985 after I graduated from Tsinghua University and was admitted to pursue a Master's degree in Shanghai. I started receiving monthly payments of about 50 yuan, an average salary for a graduate student. I could help the family a bit more at that time. ErGe and SanGe got married and had

their own children. They had six children from 1979 to 1985, which also needed more money. Weddings in Lindun and Changtai were expensive for most families in comparison to the average family income. The family needed to pay the bride's family money, which could be worth several years' income for an adult. In addition, the family needed to host banquet dinners for almost the whole neighborhood, which could cost another fortune. As all of her sons had grown up, the burden on my mother became less, and she has been living a normal widow life with us since then.

Later Life with Alzheimer's and Supernatural Farewell to Me Before Death

My mother started to have symptoms of Alzheimer's probably around 2008 when I visited her and my family from the USA. She behaved strangely by taking the bus 5 to 7 times daily from Lindun to Changtai District central town (XiangCheng). She started to receive treatment and intensive care from my family soon. **By 2010, she couldn't recognize most family members, including me. It was heartbreaking for me to see her like this**. SanGe and his wife provided most of the care during her final years. In early June 2012, I rushed back to Lindun from Columbus, USA, and saw her in bed at midnight. MS Lin, a cousin from Lindun, drove me home from Xiamen airport directly at night. Mother had just returned from the hospital in Changtai District township one day before in a specially approved ambulance. **It was a tradition in my hometown that a person had to return to their village alive before death to avoid being a lonely ghost in the afterlife.** Other villagers would refuse a dead body to be back, too. She was almost unconscious but was able to recognize me somehow. Several drops of tears burst out of her eyes when she saw me. I was told she had been waiting to see me one last time. My mother passed away in June 2012 at the age of 84, about 24 hours after I saw her in bed. **At midnight,** when she left this world, I heard a strange and loud noise from the door, shattering and vibrating for unknown reasons. I was sleeping in another house at that moment, which was about 100 meters away. In retrospect, Mother was probably saying goodbye to me that way. That was the 2nd time I personally experienced spiritual, nonphysical, and non-scientific phenomena. My mother had been the most important part of my life before 2012, especially after the passing away of my father in 1968. She lived a miserable life in her early childhood and after the loss of my father. She had a happy and normal life as a young mother and a widow from 1978 to 2008. The last family picture was taken in June 2010, including my mother and all five brothers in Lindun.

June 2010 in Lindun (From left: SiGe, Walter, SanGe, Mother, ErGe, and DaGe)

Chapter 4
Surviving Childhood in Lindun
Before 1976

4.1 Almost Given Away at Birth and Name Change After Death of Father

When I was born, my parents found my two big toes were shorter than the second toes. It was considered bad luck that my father would live a shorter life than my mother did in my hometown. **I was almost sent away at birth to other families to avoid this bad luck. My father refused. My original name was WJ Lin before 1968. It was changed to my current name after my father's death.** My name was changed at the suggestion of a local witch who said this change could prevent bad things from happening again to my family.

4.2 Almost Becoming an Orphan at Six Years Old

In 1971, when I was six years old, SiGe dislocated his elbow. My mother needed to take him to a local therapist to restore it. The therapist lived in Jiangdu village, which was about 3 km away. A good neighbor helped them to get there by riding a bicycle. On the way back, the bike fell, and my mother got hurt severely with massive bleeding. Doctors in Lindun's local clinic quickly called an ambulance and sent her to Changtai District Township Hospital for emergency medical treatment. **It was life-threatening. Mother stayed in the hospital for two days, probably with a lot of blood transfusions.** I remembered that morning SiGe and I had breakfast with the help of DaGe's wife. They were separated from us at that time by their own family, but we needed help as there was no adult at home. DaGe was working in a factory 10 km away. ErGe was joining a group of people building a railway hundreds of km away. SanGe was 12 years old, and SiGe was nine years old. When we played in the open field of the village hall that morning, we received a lot of merciful looks from nearby neighbors. Mother said that she worried most about what would happen to her young boys if she could not survive at that time. I wondered if my name change helped the family or not.

Godfather and Godmother

I had poor health as a boy probably because of (a) lack of nutritional food during my childhood. (b) my mother could not eat much when she was pregnant with all the other kids and me. (c) I was born with the Hepatitis B virus from my mother as there was no vaccine in 1965, and none of the family knew it at that time. My father had been sick with TB for three years when I was born. As a tradition in my hometown, my mother found a godfather for me after the passing away of my father. This practice was supposed to protect me from evil and improve my health. The godfather was a sworn brother of my father (结拜兄弟) named XX, who lived in the same village. He had been treated badly by local governments since 1950 because he was a bodyguard of a bandit head before 1949. Godfather had five sons who were good childhood friends of my older brothers and me. In the middle of the 1970s, I learned that I also had a Godmother in Fangyang township. Mother took me to see her one last time before she passed away.

4.3 Poor Health and Few Relatives

Severe Hemorrhoidal Bleeding at Seven Years Old in Elementary School

I had severe hemorrhoidal bleeding in school. A student saw it in the public toilet room and told my family. As no further symptoms developed, nothing was done. My mother talked about letting me have some ginseng, which would not have been the right treatment. The medical and sanitary conditions in Lindun were so bad that it was lucky for any kids like me to survive and grow up into adults.

Hospitalization Due to High Fever at Eight Years Old

I was hospitalized at Lindun Medical Clinic due to a high fever. As my mother and older brothers needed to work on the farm, I was left alone in the hospital, mostly lying in bed. After staying there for several days, I got bored and walked back home alone. It was about a 15-minute walk from the clinic to home. The physician, YM Liu, was nice and treated me well.

Few Known Relatives

I grew up without any grandparents and few relatives because of my father and mother's background. My father had a younger brother who was our only close relative. There was a distant relative from my mother's side in Yuanqian of Fangyang town and a distant cousin in the Linxi village of Lindun. Some relatives chose to avoid us after my father passed away, probably because we were too poor. My father had three sworn brothers who maintained relations with us after 1968. Two of them lived in the remote village of Wutian Mountain, which is about 1800 meters high in altitude and the highest in the Mingnan area. People can see Jinmen and Xiamen in good weather from the top of that mountain. Walking up to their village from our home took almost the whole day or more than 8 hours. When I was about ten, Mom and I visited those relatives for a wedding. We saw a giant wolf in the mountains on the way back home. Fortunately, the wolf did not notice us. SiGe and I liked visiting relatives in our childhood because that was one of the few opportunities to eat better food with meat.

4.4 Fritter Episode and Poor Custom in Hometown

Extreme Poverty

Life was primitive and hard during my childhood. There was no electricity before 1973, no running water probably until 2008, and no sewage system until now. We used nearby river water to do all the washing and cleaning. Mom needed to wash the whole family's clothes daily in the river or water channel diverted from the river, even in the wintertime. A neighborhood of about 150 people shared a well in the village. Mom needed to carry cooking and drinking water from this well probably every 2 to 3 days and store it in a big porcelain container. As there was no electricity then, we used simple kerosene lamps after dark to brighten the house so that we could see and do things such as eating dinner, doing homework, and chatting. We used a small washbasin and warm water in the wintertime to wash our faces, legs, and bodies before bed.

DaGe got married in 1969 and separated from us financially in 1970 to live his own life with his wife. Mother was left with four young sons to survive. We had only one small bedroom, about 16 square meters in area, to fit only one big bed, one small bed, one wood box, and one dresser. This was the bedroom where my father and mother got married. **Mother, SanGe, SiGe, and I slept on that king-size bed until around 1976. ErGe slept on that small twin-size bed.**

As a family without a father, life was hard for my mother, who had four children in this rural area. **I never drank milk and never had fried eggs at home in my childhood. The first time I drank milk was in 1987, at 22 years old. Meat was rare except for holidays and when there was a guest.** We raised some chickens, ducks, and pigs, primarily for sale, to have the cash to buy personal items such as clothes, textbooks, cooking oil, etc., and pay other bills. We frequently ran out of rice from April to before new rice came in July. My mom had to borrow rice from some relatives or friends; we ate sweet potatoes, taro, and home-grown vegetables. This way, we would not go hungry too much to survive. We were all malnourished and skinny because we ate little protein and did not have enough food, which led to future health issues for all of us. **I weighed less than 45kg at 1.65 meters in height before attending Tsinghua University in 1980. I still weighed less than 50kg and was 1.7 meters tall when I graduated from Tsinghua University in 1985.** My mom was very good at growing different kinds of vegetables, and I used to help water them daily with my brothers. There was a market fair once a week in downtown Lindun. This was a good time to sell vegetables and other items for valuable cash. I sometimes helped Mother sell, and I felt awkward when classmates from the school visited our booth.

In my family, new clothes were only allowed during Chinese New Year. Most of the time, I wore old clothes from my older brothers. I walked barefoot almost all the time, even in winter, and almost in all activities, including working in the farm field, cutting tree branches and bushes in the mountains, and attending physical education classes in school. **I still ran 100 meters barefoot when I went to high school and even in my 1st year at Tsinghua University, which surprised many people, including my teachers.**

I never had toys when I was a boy and dreamed of having one. DaGe and his wife had separated from us financially and lived their own life around 1970. My nephew, who was probably two to three years old, got toys like small plastic balloons and plastic water guns from his parents for Chinese New Year. I was about six to seven years old then. I envied him so much and wanted to play with him so I could play with those toys a bit. I did not dare to ask my mother for these toys as I knew we were too poor to even think about them.

I used to go to the so-called daycare organized by the village, so my mom could go to work on the farm. There was no charge for daycare because it was still a public enterprise (公社). The daycare teachers were young people from Zhangzhou City sent to rural areas for re-education during the Cultural Revolution from 1968 to 1975. It was fun to play with many kids my age at that time. Public enterprises collectively owned the farm field. Almost all adults and teenagers as young as 12 years old, like SanGe or above, went to work on farms to earn some credits for possible future income. People did not know how much they could earn until the end of the farming season when all crops were harvested and sold. Therefore, each person had to do his best to participate in the assigned work each day when there was no rain to earn more credit hours. When the weather was bad that day, they had to stay home without income. As I remember, an adult over 18, like ErGe, could earn ten credit hours daily by working at least 10 hours. **The income in a good year was about 0.5 Yuan RMB per day in 1972. One kg of pork meat cost about 1.5 Yuan at that time. I started 1st grade in 1971 when I was only six years old so my mom could have more time working in farming and earn some income**. She could earn about 70% of an adult male's earnings as a mother with smaller kids. Because I attended the school too young, I was not mature enough to understand some lectures, especially Pingying, though I did well in math.

No Birthday Celebration We never had any birthday celebrations in my family as we were too poor, which led me to this habit of no birthday parties when I had my own family and kids in the USA. I did not even know for a long time that birthdays were something to be celebrated with a party, as we always lived in survival mode. I did not know my exact birthday until 1980 when I needed to fill out forms at Tsinghua University.

Fritters Episode and Frugal Childhood I tried to help my family when I was ten years old besides doing housework. One day, I collected sellable items from the public garbage places near stores and clinics in the downtown area of Lindun with a friend. We got a small amount of money by selling those items. A small cafeteria was nearby selling fritters (油条), which smelled so good that my friend suggested we buy one using the money we had just earned. Each fritter cost about 3 cents (RMB) at that time. Some of my neighbors saw this and informed my mother later. When I got home that evening, my mother quietly told me that I should not do that as what I did could make it difficult for our family to seek help from others. Neighbors might complain that your kids were spending on luxury food like fritters while your family was trying to borrow money or rice from others. **I listened, understood, and then dropped down my head. I felt guilty and never did it again.** Similar events occurred several times when I ate my food outside in the evening with my childhood friends. Mother gave me more rice in the rice porridge as I was the youngest kid, while she and my older brothers chose to eat more sweet potatoes with more diluted porridge. Some neighbors complained to my mother that our porridge was too thick with too much rice, so that was why our family needed to borrow rice from others before the harvest season. **From that moment, I became cautious about spending money on unnecessary items, including eating out in China and later in the USA.**

Close Brotherhood ErGe, Sange, SiGe, and I became very close as we slept in that tiny bedroom with Mother. One of the funniest things for me as a boy was playing a card game called "40 points" with them while we all sat on this big, king-size bed. I learned very quickly and could calculate and predict the game at the very young age of seven. This probably laid a good foundation for my math and logical analysis capacity, including future Bridge games at Tsinghua and Shanghai during tournaments. SiGe and I also worked together frequently to catch loach from the water channel diverted from the river. The river was about 80 meters wide. A small water channel about 3 meters wide was built long ago to divert water into our village so we could wash vegetables and clothes near our home. The water channel was several hundred meters long from the river. A lot of loaches swim down the channel in the spring season. SiGe and I made a net ourselves. We just put the net into the channel, waited for a while, and harvested every 10 to 20 minutes. Sometimes, we could have one to two kgs of loaches in one day, which were good supplementary proteins for our family. Too many kids were doing that, and we had to limit to a net every five meters away. Whoever went upstream usually caught more, so each person needed to get there early to occupy a better spot. The cooking was easy. We cleaned the loaches in water and put them in a hot pot with salt for 30 minutes. They were delicious to eat with rice or without rice. SanGe and I sometimes went to nearby mountains to dig bamboo. It was done during rainy days as the soil became soft enough to dig in.

Sacrifice of ErGe and SanGe SanGe dropped out of elementary school in 4th grade when he was only 11 years old because we were too poor. He needed to help the family by working full-time on a farm to earn more credits. I remember the teacher visiting my home several times and trying to persuade my mother to let SanGe continue schooling. SanGe was shy and hid when the teacher came. Though public education was free, there were still fees for textbooks, pens, pencils, and notebooks, which were still a burden to my family for each kid. By that time, ErGe had dropped out of high school right after my father passed away in 1968. ErGe and SanGe were very smart students and should have been able to attend college if my family's economic conditions had not been so bad. **I have felt indebted to them as both of them sacrificed themselves**

and supported SiGe and me so that we could continue our education through college. They raised me together with my mother. This was why I had done my best to help my brothers financially after I started to have income in 1985, especially when their kids went to college.

Poor Custom in Hometown At that time, in Lindun and Changtai, the Husband's family needed to pay the wife's family a lump sum of money as a wedding gift, which could be up to more than multiple years' of family income. The husband's family was also expected to have a banquet inviting all relatives and neighbors, which would cost another fortune. **When DaGe got married, my mother needed to go to multiple families to borrow money with a lantern at night for the wedding money up to 360 Yuan, putting the whole family in debt for many years before being paid back.** When there were events like a wedding or the birth of a newborn from neighbors and relatives, people were expected to give some gifts or cash. **In my memory, my mother was constantly worried about where to find the money for this kind of event, especially for the weddings of ErGe and SanGe.** Therefore, I was quite resentful of these bad customs and old traditions in my hometown, which hurt many poor families like ours. I tried to avoid them as best as I could.

4.5 Childhood Friends and Farming at The Early Age of 10

There were a dozen kids close to my age in our neighborhood. We played and studied from the daycare to the Lindun Central Elementary School. Among them, SiGe, FQ Liu, and I were lucky to attend college later. All others remained in Lindun as peasants. During that period, students were asked to do a lot of physical labor in school, like farming, to help raise income for the school. We needed to plant tea trees, sugar cane, or other plants in the nearby hills, which took us about one hour to walk one way. After school, I had to help with a lot of housework daily, including cooking dinner, feeding pigs and livestock, and growing vegetables in a small piece of self-retained land with SiGe. I also started light farming work at about ten during the summer and weekends, like harvesting rice, peanuts, and sugar cane and moving cow and pig dung to farm fields. From probably 1975, I needed to go to nearby mountains to cut tree branches and bushes each weekend so they could be used for cooking after they were dried. There was no coal and natural gas in my village and Changtai. I mainly went with SiGe and sometimes with other kids near my age group, like FQ Liu, JY Xie, and FR Liu et al.

Childhood Activities in Lindun

As a young boy, I often liked to follow SiGe and his friends, including JY Xie and FQ Liu. We fought a lot, like most young brothers of similar ages. Sometimes, I complained to Mom, and SiGe would get disciplined. There was a student entertainment team at Lindun Central Elementary School. SiGe and JY Xie were part of it with Amelia, my elementary school classmate, who became my wife in 1991. I envied them a lot at that time because they had opportunities to do that kind of performance, often in different villages. More importantly, they got to have good meals like rice porridge with a lot of pork belly and vegetables after the performance.

We used to swim a lot in the river during the summer season. There were no factories and pollution then, so the water was clean and full of fish. We could catch fish at night by searching under the rocks.

We also played a lot of table tennis in school. The school had several concrete tables without nets. We just put two rocks in the middle and a wood stick above the rock to act as a net. SiGe and I could not afford a real table tennis racket and needed to make one from a wood plate. I liked and played quite well in table tennis, mainly after school. Sometimes, I played too long and missed helping with housework on time. Lindun Central School had several excellent players like FX Lin and LL Liu. FX Lin was in the same grade as SanGe. He won a championship in a tournament in Changtai District and probably later in Zhangzhou City.

In the early 1970s, in elementary school, most kids were required to become little red guards. For context, Changtai and Fujian were close to Taiwan, which is still separated from mainland China now due to the civil war between the Nationalist Party and the Communist Party from 1945 to 1949. After the war, about four million people retreated from mainland China to Taiwan with the Nationalist Party. Many families have been separated since 1949 for a long time. The oldest uncle of my wife, Amelia, went to Taiwan in 1949 at age 29 and did not return home until he was 95 years old with his two daughters. 80% of the people on Taiwan Island before 1949 came from Fujian Province and spoke the Minnan dialect. Minnan dialect is mainly spoken in the cities such as Xiamen, Zhangzhou, and Quanzhou in South Fujian Province. It is also spoken in Santou of Guangdong Province and some Hainan and Zhejiang Province areas. Little Red Guards did many weird things, like monitoring village people suspected of being connected to the Nationalist Party at night. The school even organized a parade for students and gathered them at the houses of those families to protest their routine activities. One of those families was Amelia's aunt, her father's older sister. Her aunt married a man whose father and uncle were senior officials in the Nationalist government before 1949. The father, CJ Liang, was Changtai District commissioner before 1949 under the nationalist party. His uncle, HY Liang, who escaped to Taiwan in 1949, was a major general under the Nationalist government. This uncle graduated from the well-known HuangPu military school in Guangdong, where Jiang Jieshi was president. Jiang Jieshi was eventually the president of China, including mainland China and Taiwan, before 1949. Our elementary school organized a demonstration at the home of Amelia's aunt because they killed a live chicken to eat, which was normal in rural areas. Her aunt's family was accused of giving a warning to a monkey by killing a chicken (杀鸡敬猴).

There were balloons with candies and fliers from Jinmen Island, which was still under the control of the Nationalist Party from Taiwan. We were told not to keep those items if we found them in mountains and farming fields.

The only entertainment in Lindun then was the local government's public movies. There would be an announcement if a film would be played in the village outdoor square. Villagers needed to bring their chairs or benches. All the kids would be excited for the whole day and ask their parents to get them to watch the movie at night. Each family would eat supper earlier and could occupy a better front spot before the screen. There were only limited movies nationwide like "The Legend of the Red Lantern" (红灯记),"Tunnel Warfare"(地道战) "Flower Selling Girl" (卖花姑娘), "Red Detachment of Women" (红色娘子军), "Shajiaban" (沙家浜), "Railway Guerrillas" (铁道游击队). Most of the time, when I was very young, I would fall asleep while watching movies on my mother's back. When I was old enough, I would watch movies with other kids. We often watched the same film multiple times, as it was shown in different villages like Shiheng, Linxi, and Jiaomei. We needed to walk up to 30 to 45 minutes to watch a movie at night.

Only trip Outside Changtai before 1976. I was in Lindun and Fangyang most of the time before I graduated from elementary school, except for one trip to Jimei of Xiamen around 1975. I unexpectedly got five yuan somewhere, which was much money then. FR Liu's family had a distant relative in Jimei's rural area and needed to visit them for a family matter. I asked him if I could travel with him as I had that precious five Yuan. Surprisingly, FR Liu, his family, and my mom agreed. They asked if I could bring some raw rice with us as we probably would stay there for two nights. We took a bus to Tongan District town first and switched to another bus to Jimei. We then had to walk a long distance to reach the home of FR's relative. I was excited to see the ocean for the first time, even though it was only 30 km from Lindun. We also visited the monument of Chen Jiageng, a well-known person in Fujian and China, for his outstanding contributions to education in Xiamen and the support of China from Singapore and Malaysia during World War II. He was the founder of Xiamen and Jimei Universities.

4.6 Almost Dropping Out of Elementary School

I almost dropped out of the elementary school in the spring of 1976. At 11 years old, I was required to do much housework during school seasons, like cooking, feeding pigs, chickens, and ducks, and helping mom grow vegetables after school. During weekends, SiGe and I had to go up to the mountain areas to cut and collect tree branches for cooking for the whole family. My mom was stern and strict with a lousy temper, well known in our neighborhood, probably because of the enormous pressure of life without my father. We were told we needed to work if we wanted to eat, a tradition in rural areas. My mom herself had grown up with that kind of discipline. I loved to play table tennis. Sometimes, I played too long after school and forgot the housework at home. I would then receive strong discipline from my mother. **I quit school briefly because of the harsh life at home. During that time, I went to dig bush roots in the nearby hills, which could be sold for money after being cut into small pieces and dried.** I sometimes accidentally dug into someone's graveyard, which was bad luck. Snakes were expected to be seen in the mountain areas as Changtai was in warm and humid southern regions full of trees and bushes. One day, the head teacher of my class came to my home and asked me to go back to school with my mom's support. **On the 2nd day, I went to work in the mountain again and saw a big golden wolf on the mountain hill, which was close to my father's graveyard.** Even though that wolf did not see me from a far distance of about 100 meters, **I got scared in that quiet mountain area as I was alone. I quickly ran home and returned to school.**

I graduated from Lindun Elementary School in the summer of 1976. It was also called Lindun Wuqi School at that time. The following class photo was found among a few remaining items left by my mother when she passed away in 2012. This was also the earliest photo I could find of myself. There were 52 graduates. Amelia was 5th from left in the front row.

Elementary School Graduation Class Photo in 1976 (Walter at 6th from Right at Last Row)

Amelia and I were probably the only two able to attend a four-year college later. It was hard to imagine then that we would get married later and have two wonderful children. Amelia's parents had quite good jobs compared to most of the Lindun and Changtai families. Her father was a teacher, and her mother was a salaried staff in the local township. They lived a much better life than my family in 1976. My family's income and social status were probably at the very bottom of society in China, and Changtai then.

Chapter 5
Two-Year Middle School in Lindun

5.1 Table Tennis Tournament in Changtai

I had my two-year middle school from September 1976 to June 1978 at Lindun Central Middle School, the exact location of the elementary school. In the first year of middle school, I continued playing a lot of table tennis in school after the class. One day, while working in the farm field, my teacher suddenly stopped by and asked me to play in a table tennis tournament for the school as I was still under 12. The tournament lasted several days in Fangyang, about seven kilometers from Lindun. I got to eat good food provided in the tournament, with many dishes I had never had at home. **That was the first time I ate fried eggs** because my mother had to sell our eggs in the market to have badly needed cash. I played well and won the tournament among all the middle schools in Fangyang township. Lindun was part of Fangyang township at that time. As a champion, I represented the Fangyang School area several weeks later to play in a bigger Changtai District School tournament. The tournament was held in Fufan village of ChenXian Township, which was about 30 Km away from Lindun. I was so excited to be in a place I never visited before. More importantly, the food they provided was much better than at home. **It was my first time eating a cake made of egg and flour.** I did well in the individual contest and won 2nd place by beating many good players from different school districts. Some of them had received many years of semi-professional training at Changtai District Tennis Club. BW Tu won the championship and later attended the tournament in Zhangzhou City. He won the championship again among all school districts in Zhangzhou. I heard he also participated in the tournament in Fujian Province, representing Zhangzhou City, and won a ranked position later in the top three. He and I became friends and kept in contact for a while.

5.2 Restoration of GaoKao and ZhongKao in 1977

Den Xiaoping returned to be the national leader in 1976 and restored the National College Entrance Exam, called GaoKao and ZhongKao, in 1977. This greatly impacted our generation and the previous one. Millions of young people started studying hard to grasp this golden opportunity to attend college. This was the only chance for people like my family to change their lives: leave rural areas, attend college, and find a job in the city. At that time, more than 90% of the population in China lived in the rural countryside, which had a much poorer lifestyle than those living in the city or those having a steady salary income as a teacher in rural areas. All schools mobilized teachers and students to prepare for these sacred National Exams. GaoKao was for those planning to apply for four-year or three-year colleges. The four-year college was also called BenKe, and the three-year college was called Dazhuang. GaoKao was for high school graduates and millions who missed this opportunity during the 10-year cultural revolution. ZhongKao was for those wanting to attend high school or two-year colleges (ZhongZhuang), like middle school graduates and millions of youths who missed opportunities from 1966 to 1976. One day in the fall of 1977, the school gathered all students and teachers to announce that one of our high school graduates, SQ Lin from Jiandu village, was accepted into Xiamen University. Our school location housed Changtai 3rd High School, Lindun Middle School, and Lindun Central Elementary School then. There were several good teachers in this high school. Due to the cultural revolution, they were sent to Lindun from major cities to reeducate in rural areas. Some graduated from good universities like Beijing University, Xiamen University, Beijing Telecommunication University, and Fujian Normal University. Before coming to this school, one or two were faculty in Xiamen and other universities. That was one of the reasons our town produced many good high school graduates in the years after 1977.

SiGe was one grade above me. Both of us started studying very hard in the fall of 1977. My neighbors later joked that SiGe and I always studied and read loudly in the early morning by the big tree at the front of our home and the water channel. That water channel was used to wash clothes and clean vegetables in the morning. Most of my middle school teachers had only high school diplomas. They were preparing themselves to attend either GaoKao or ZhongKao exams. They were dedicated teachers. I ran into one of my middle school teachers later in Xiangcheng while studying in Changtai No. 1. High school in 1979. That teacher was selling soy sauce and salted vegetables in a public-owned store. He did not get into college at that time. Each class's teacher wanted students to spend more time in their class. In the spring of 1978, I was chosen to live in the dorm as one of the better students, even though my home was only a 10-minute walk away from school. The dorm was converted from a big classroom which accommodated about 30 students. It was one of the classrooms behind that graduation class photo in 1976. The school and teachers wanted those students to study days and nights in school. I should mention that most of my teachers, like FH Lin and ZW Xie, were very nice to me, probably because I was one of the best students in the school that year. Many of my teachers were classmates of my older brothers, which might have helped. I showed much interest and passion in classes like math, physics, and chemistry, and I was fascinated with Newton's laws, science, and logistic analysis. At that time in China, there was a slogan that read, "You can go everywhere in the world without fear if you learn well in math, physics, and chemistry."

One of my classmates, JK Liu, quit school because of a bad family situation. It was a pity to see this as he was one of the best students in my middle school class. Several years later, SanGe married a girl from YuanQian, a small village in Fangyang. I learned that she and JK were cousins. JK's father was her uncle from her mother's side. JK eventually became a peasant and opened a small stone refining shop like most people did in Lindun. He got married and lived a typical life as a peasant in Lindun.

5.3 Almost Did Not Go to High School

Middle school candidates were then asked to attend either high school or ZhongZhuan (two-year college) before taking the ZhongKao exam. **DaGe wanted me to go to a two-year college to graduate and make money soon at 15.** However, as the best student in my grade, all of my teachers suggested that I go to high school to have a chance to attend a four-year college later. I eventually chose a high school, disappointing DaGe.

In June of 1978, I participated in Zhongkao and achieved an excellent score. I was selected as one of the best high school students to attend Changtai No. 1 High School in a particular class (重点班). About 45 students from the whole district were selected based on their ZhongKao scores. The district gathered the best high school teachers from all schools in each subject to teach this class. The subjects included Math, Physics, Chemistry, Chinese Language, History and English. I heard later that my ZhongKao score was higher than most of my teachers who also participated in that year's exam. I had to move from Lindun to live in Xiangcheng in September 1978 when I was only 13 years old. I had never visited Xiangcheng (县城) before and was excited about this opportunity to live there. At that time, in poor rural areas like Fangyang and Lindun, there was a saying that you would go hungry if you could visit Xiangcheng. **I did not realize that I had to start** living independently, away from my hometown and birthplace, from that time at such a young age. SiGe was unhappy as he still needed to live in Lindun to attend high school.

Chapter 6
Two-Year High School in Changtai District Town

I spent two years in high school, from August 1978 to June 1980. Among the 45 students in this particular class, six were from Fangyang, including Lindun. They were JY He, FJ He, JW Gao, FL He, JB Liu, and me. JB was from Jiandu of LinDun. FL was from KeShan. JY and FJ were from ChiLing of Fangyang. Those students with urban residency had better living conditions. I realized again that my family belonged to the bottom part of society and that I needed to work hard to improve myself.

As a socialist country, China provided free education with tuition and boarding in the 1970s and 1980s, from daycare and elementary school to college, even though the country was impoverished. It also provided financial aid for poor college students so they could pay for food, clothes, and other things. That was one of the reasons the college admittance rate was so low from 1977 to 1980, as the country had a limited budget **I have been grateful for this system that allowed me to finish my high school, undergraduate, and graduate studies in China before 1988**.

Life in high school was poor and challenging with primitive conditions, which I did not quite mind as a poor student at that time, as living conditions were similarly bad at home. Instead, I was excited to have this opportunity to study in this particular class. I followed all student rules well and studied hard, including on weekends. I moved up to become one of the best students in this class in 2nd semester. I continued excelling in physics, chemistry, math, history, and political science. For some reason, I could have almost perfect scores on history and political science on every significant test because I could memorize nearly every page, even every paragraph of the whole textbook. This capability continued into college, which allowed me to do well in this kind of class that required good memory. I was not quite as strong in Chinese language class. The teacher of this class declared to the whole class that I could be admitted into a 4-year college if I could have just 60% points in Chinese GaoKao, as I did so well in other subjects.

The high school had a big cafeteria where all students could prepare meals. We all brought raw rice from home. Breakfast was porridge from the cafeteria. For lunch and dinner, we needed to put uncooked rice with water in a small personal metal box (饭盒) ahead of time and give it to the cafeteria staff to put into a giant steam container. Most rural students like me also brought dishes to eat with rice as it was too expensive to buy from the cafeteria. They included dried and salted white carrots and vegetables, which could last many weeks without going bad, as Changtai was always warm. It would be lucky to have a bit of pork mixed with those dishes. As there was not enough rice for my family, I always needed to put more water in the box so it would look like eating porridge. Indeed, we would put sweet potato in, too. We also brought a hot water container (热水瓶) or thermos) to get hot water from the cafeteria during meal hours. There was also a place near the cafeteria where students could wash their clothes with water. We needed to bring a washbasin (脸盆) to wash clothes. This washbasin was also used to wash our bodies with hot water in the dorm, as the town had no dedicated bathroom. The wet clothes were hung on a long rope outside the dorm when it was not raining.

I was very skinny and malnourished, with less than 45 kg in weight and 1.65 meters in height then. I did not perform well in physical education class, like throwing the shot put

(扔铅球), which required power and strength. The teacher was nice enough to let me pass after I tried very hard several times. Most of the time, I wore flip-flops all day as regular shoes were expensive. In track and field class, I ran barefoot.

6.1 Living in an Auditorium Theatre with 300 Students

In my first year of high school, I lived in a dorm converted from an old auditorium theatre for more than 300 high school students from different towns. There was a big public toilet outside the auditorium. Hundreds of double-layer wood beds were jammed into this huge auditorium. I lived in a lower bed in this big dorm at that time. **Some window glass was broken, and windows were not entirely sealed. We could feel cold air blowing into the dorm during winter.** Each student could put their belongings in a suitcase, usually made of wood, to store personal belongings like clothes and food. The suitcase was put on the floor. Mice were frequently seen on the ground floor because of the food wasted in that auditorium. We moved into a smaller dorm converted from a standard classroom in 2nd year, similar to when I lived in Lindun Central School in 1977. There were about 38 male students in our particular class in this dorm. The building conditions were better, and the windows were better sealed.

6.2 Strict Schedule and Nice Teachers at High School

We had classes in the classrooms Monday to Saturday from 8:00 am to 12:00 pm and 1:00 pm to 5:00 pm. There was a one-hour lunch break. After dinner, we were also required to go to the classrooms for homework and study from around 7:00 pm to 10:00 pm. Each morning around 7:00 am, one physical education teacher would come to our dorm to wake students up to go to morning physical exercise, like running, before we had breakfast. This teacher would also come to ask students to do physical exercise before dinner around 6:00 pm. Sunday was free of classes. However, most of our class, especially those from rural areas, still studied in dorms or classrooms. I usually only went home after the semester ended, as it was 37 km from XiangCheng to Lindun. A bus ticket to go home on weekends was expensive. SanGe regularly brought rice and vegetable dishes to me by biking from Lindun to Xiangcheng during the school semester. **Once, I needed to return to Xiangcheng from Lindun, and our family ran out of money for me on bus tickets and other things. SanGe and I went to a neighbor, JS Liu, to borrow five Yuan so that I could come back to high school. We both waited in his home for a while to get the money.** JS was an elementary school teacher and was considered a better-off family in our village because his family recently received a reimbursement from the local government. The reimbursement was to cover his family's loss since 1956 because the local government wrongly confiscated their personal property. That occurred due to his poor family status, defined in 1950 as a wealthy peasant (富农). A one-way bus ticket cost about 0.50 Yuan from Lindun to Xiangcheng then. My family paid him back after selling some vegetables and eggs later.

Almost all teachers in the high school treated me very well. They were the best high teachers in Changtai District at that time. The following were a few names: ZJ Liu in Math, TS Chen in Physics, SC Fang in Chemistry, TY Yue in Chinese Language, and XS Ye in Political Science. TS Chen and SC Fang were also headteachers (班主任). The wife of XS Ye was Doctor YM Liu, who was in the Lindun clinic for many years and knew my family well as a colleague of my father. SC Fang passed away relatively young in my 2nd year of high school due to liver cancer. Most high school students, including our class, attended his funeral. He was knowledgeable, caring for all students, and well-respected in class. TS Chen was also the physics teacher for SiGe in Meipeng, and became our physics teacher in my 2nd year of high school. He was very nice to me. FH Lin, who was in Lindun Central School, transferred to our high school as the chief of the supporting department soon after I moved to Xiangcheng. He had a single dorm of about 12 square meters as the high school's chief supporting staff. He nicely gave one of his keys to me so I could study there whenever he was out of town. YM Yuan was a teacher of SiGe. His wife was a nurse at Lindun Clinic and a colleague of my father. One night, I ran out of hot water and was so thirsty that I went to the laundry area to get some tap water. It happened that his wife was washing clothes over there. She asked me to go to her home to get some boiled water. I gradually realized that she might be the nurse who used to work with my father at Lindun Clinic. She worked over there for many years after 1968. After I told her who I was and my father's name, she recalled and was excited to introduce me to her husband.

6.3 Surprise Special Meal Treatment from School

Sometimes, in the last semester of high school, I was suddenly informed that I was awarded special meal treatment to be allowed to have meals with teachers funded by the high school. They included breakfast, lunch, and dinner from around March 1980 to July 1980, right before GaoKao. I did not have to eat porridge and sweet potato together with dried salted carrots and vegetables(咸菜萝卜干) from then on in high school. The meals were much better. **From that moment, I had more and better food to eat without going hungry.** There was meat in the meal almost every day, which was unimaginable for me then. More importantly, they were paid for by the high school and cost at least 10 Yuans per month. 10 Yuan was equivalent to the total monthly income of an adult male peasant in Lindun. I learned later from SanGe that the high school sent people directly to my village back in Lindun to investigate my family's economic situation. They confirmed that my family belonged to one of the poorest families in Changtai District. The school decided to provide financial support to me through daily meals. I was the only one in my class and probably the whole high school to receive this award, as I did not see any other students when I had meals with those teachers. **In December of 1999, when I first came back to Changtai after eight years of studying and working in the USA, I donated a certain amount of money to the Changtai Educational Department to show my appreciation for the help I received back in those years.** This department oversaw Changtai No. 1 High School and Lindun Central Middle and Elementary School. I hoped they could use that money to help students from poor families. **During that trip, I invited neighbors and childhood friends in Lindun for a nice free dinner, asking them not to bring us gifts, food, drink, or cash (Hongbao).**

Good Classmates and Friends I had several good classmates and friends from high school. Almost all my classmates were very good to me, probably because of my easygoing personality, good academic performance, and willingness to help them whenever they had questions. Sometimes, in the 2nd year of high school, I had to spend most of my time during night sessions helping and answering questions from classmates. To finish my homework, I had to find a quiet place to study, like the dorm of Teacher FH Lin or other locations.MS Shen, who was also one of the best students in this class, was a good friend of mine. He was the best math student in our class. He lived in Xiangcheng. His father was an accountant in a factory in Yangxi town, and his mother worked in a local store selling food like salted vegetables (酱瓜). I ran into her once when I was out of salted vegetables from home and had to refill in that store. **I first tasted dumplings in MS's house and was amazed at their deliciousness.** HL Liu joined our class in the 2nd year from Huaan County. His father was the principal of Lindun Elementary School. His mother also taught in that school. She was born and grew up in Shiheng village too. HL's older brothers played table tennis with me together back in Lindun before 1978. So naturally, we became good friends quickly. GQ Ye from Gulong Town was very nice to me. He brought goose meat to me several times from his home, probably after seeing me overeating salted vegetables and dried carrots. He came also from a peasant family. I am still grateful for the generosity of him and his family

6.4 Taking GaoKao Exam One Year Earlier Than Normal Students

In 1980, there were six classes in the sophomore year in Changtai No. 1 High School. Our class was a specially selected one that was allowed to participate in GaoKao in the 2nd year, one year earlier, while the remaining five classes needed to wait until they were in the 3rd year. Our class was split in the 2nd year as students needed to choose to go into STEM or liberal arts directions. The majority of students chose STEM as there were more job opportunities. For STEM direction, six subjects were to be tested: Math, Physics, Chemistry, Chinese Language, Political Science, and English. Few people knew English well then, and it wasn't easy to find qualified English teachers. Only 30% was accounted in total score for English in 1980. It took three days to finish GaoKao. There were morning and afternoon sections each day, which lasted about 3 hours every section.

High School Graduation Class Photo in 1980 (Walter at 1ˢᵗ of the first Row from Left)

At that time, we were required to enter a list of five universities to be considered for admittance before GaoKao, based on our past performances and predictions. The college admittance rate in 1980 was about 3% nationwide in China. Therefore, picking the correct university list was critical to my success and future career. If you put the better universities on your list and were not admitted, you had to wait another year to participate in next year's GaoKao. If you were admitted into a university and did not want to attend, you also needed to wait for next year's GaoKao. Most students, especially those from poor families, would be conservative in picking less strong universities so they could get into them first. I was advised to select SJTU (Shanghai Jiaotong University) first because (a) It was one of the best ten universities in China in 1980. (b) A teacher from SJTU came to recruit high school students from Zhangzhou City in 1980. He happened to have graduated from Changtai No. 1 High School before and was a student of my high school teachers, ZJ Liu and TS Chen. My teachers even introduced me to him before GaoKao. (c) Shanghai is located in southern China. The climate and food style are not very different from those in Changtai. So naturally, I expected to be accepted into SJTU if I performed well in GaoKao. After finishing GaoKao in June 1980, I went home directly to work in the farming field. I still do not have my physical high school diploma, as nobody has informed me where to pick it up. The attached high school graduation class photo was provided in November 2022 by a high school classmate. I was the 1st from left at the bottom row because I was one of the shortest in the class.

6.5 Summer Work in Lindun's Farm Field

Summer was the busiest time for peasants in Lindun and Changtai. They needed to get up before dawn. After having a simple breakfast, like porridge with sweet potato, peasants would work in the rice field until it was dark to come home. There was a short lunch break in the farming field. They needed to harvest the mature rice in June, which could be dried in open fields. The rice field needed to be rebuilt quickly to be planted for the next season's rice again within one month. This way, peasants could have another season of rice to be harvested in the Fall. This was the so-called double harvest and double plant season (双收双种). The season usually lasted for about two months during the summer school break. **I was fully involved during the summer breaks of 1977 to 1980 when I was a bit older, aged 11 to 15. I had better capability then and wanted to help. It was challenging work, 12 hours per day and seven days per week for over two months. This kind of work experience provided me with a persistent spirit and training to overcome any hardship I faced during the future journey from Lindun to Columbus.** At that time, I could see that my mother was getting older and weaker. She started to prepare meals for us at home mostly. SanGe, SiGe, and I worked full-time in the farming field. ErGe worked in a factory at that time. I wanted to prove to my mom that her son was growing up and could contribute to reducing her burden. Rice fields could be full of water with fish, crabs, snakes, and leeches as no fertilizer or weed killer was available and used then. Snakes would run away when people started getting into the rice field. Leech was common and difficult to avoid. It was hard to remove them by hand, but better with a knife that was used to cut rice plants. Sometimes, people had a dozen leeches on their legs after getting off the rice field. Another primary task for teenagers like me to help farming was shipping cow and pig dung to farm fields with bare hands, bare feet, and no mask. Though they smelled bad in the summertime, they were the best organic fertilizer for rice fields. We also cut and collected bushes and leaves from nearby areas and put them in the farming field to let them rot and become fertilizer. In addition to rice, our family grew peanuts and sugar cane. Wheat was not popular as Lindun's climate was too warm. Raw peanuts can be eaten, but they can easily lead to diarrhea. It tasted better to cook first. It was fun for kids to harvest sugar cane as we could eat them simultaneously. Sometimes, there were worms inside sugar canes when you chewed them. Sugar canes were shipped to a nearby factory in Yuanxi town to produce sugar.

Chapter 7
Undergraduate at Tsinghua University from 1980 to 1985

7.1 Surprised Admittance Notice from Tsinghua University

In the summer of 1980, when I was working in the farming field, **I surprisingly received an admittance notice (录取通知书) from Tsinghua University even though I had not placed this university on my application list.** My family was happy that I could go to any college and migrate away from a rural area to a city from now on. During that period, that was the only way for me to escape from the rural area of being a peasant and have a city residence (城市户口) in China. In the 1980s, more than 90% of the population in China lived in rural areas and held a peasant residency. Less than 10% of people held city residency, which had superior advantages over those with peasant residency. People with peasant residency could not apply for jobs outside rural farming areas. Their children could not attend schools in cities with much better education resources. Travel with a rural residency might be restricted too, similar to current North Korea. People needed to get a written permit from the village headquarters before traveling into major cities, especially those far away from your area, to stay in a motel and buy tickets for buses or trains.

Tsinghua University has been a dream university for millions of young people and high school students in China. Most students would not dare to apply for this university because it was so difficult to get in, like a lottery. I was not super excited to be admitted into Tsinghua when I received the admittance notice. Tsinghua University is located in

Beijing, which was much colder and would cost more for me to travel there. Later on, I suspected that Tsinghua and Beijing University had privileges over other universities in picking whoever students they wanted ahead of time. Tsinghua picked me probably because (a) I was one of the youngest high school graduates to be admitted into this university at 15 years old. (b) I came from an impoverished family background and should have an excellent potential to grow (c) I suspected teachers in Changtai No.1 High School and even the Changtai Education Department (教育局) might lobby or promote me to Tsinghua because they badly wanted a Changtai graduate to be admitted into Tsinghua. **No one in Changtai District had been officially accepted into Tsinghua University before 1980.** I became a public figure in Changtai District because I broke the district's history, which was considered a poor agricultural district in Fujian. From 1977 to 1980, the admittance rate of GaoKao was less than 3% to 5%, depending on the provinces. Only about ten students of our specially selected class of 45 were admitted into colleges in 1980. Some of them went to DaZhuan (大专). Most of my high school classmates needed to study one more year and were able to get into colleges in 1981.

In 1980, Tsinghua admitted 2000 students nationwide. Among these students, 600 were probably from Beijing, and 80 were from Fujian. Fujian Province had a population of more than 30 million then, which was three times more than the population of Beijing City in 1980. There are more than 60 counties in Fujian. Usually, there were better high schools with much better educational resources in Fuzhou and Xiamen, two major cities in Fujian Province. Hence, more students over there could go to Tsinghua. Though GaoKao has been one of China's cleanest and most non-corrupt processes for millions of poor youths to escape poverty and move up in their life, the fairness of its admittance quote policy for different regions is still under debate. People question why so many students are admitted into well-known universities like Tsinghua University, Beijing University, Shanghai Jiaotong University, and Fudan University from major cities such as Beijing and Shanghai. This is especially unfair to big provinces like Henan, Shandong, and Jiangxi since there were not enough good universities in their regions. Some parents give up good jobs in those regions to move into major cities like Beijing and Shanghai to have better opportunities for their children to get into good universities.

7.2 Unforgettable Three-Day Trip Alone at 15 Years Old to Tsinghua Campus

Beijing, located 2800 km away, was a remote and strange place for me, as shown on the map of China. I had no idea how to get there by myself. Someone in Changtai Education Department (教育局) told me to take a train first from the Guokeng railway station to Laizhou, a small railway station in northern Fujian close to Naping city as shown on the map of Fujian. There was a direct train from Fuzhou City to Beijing, and I could catch that train in Laizhou close to midnight. A lot needed to be prepared, including money, winter clothes, and a quilt (被子). I obtained the paperwork to transfer my rural residency from Shiheng village of Lindun to get a city residency in Tsinghua. Many colleagues from ErGe's factory donated two to five Yuan to help with my trip. One sworn brother of DaGe also lent me 30 Yuans, which I regretted many years later. A carpenter in ErGe's factory made a wooden case for me to store personal items in Tsinghua. I never took a train before. I needed to travel 2800 km (1750 miles) for almost three days, primarily by myself, on the road from Lindun to Beijing.

At the end of August 1980, I said goodbye to my mother and other family members in Lindun and took a bus with SiGe to Guokeng railroad station, about 30 km away. SiGe needed to go to his college in Sanming. We shipped that wooden case with a big quilt to Tsinghua directly from the railway station. I brought two bags of personal items with me. We embarked on this train in the afternoon at about 2:00 pm and arrived in Sanming around 6:00 pm. SiGe got off the train, and I was now on that train to Laizhou myself. I usually spoke the MingNan dialect before and barely spoke official Mandarin (普通话) for a whole day in Changai. There are a dozen local dialects in Fujian alone and probably more than 200 in China. Each region, like Sanming, Putian, and Fuzhou, has its local dialect. So, people must speak official Mandarin to communicate while away from their region or using public transportation tools like trains. I had no choice but to speak Mandarin officially on that train. **I was very nervous about missing this stop at Laizhou as the train would go to Fuzhou if I did not get off on time.** By 10:00 pm, the train arrived in Laizhou, a tiny railway station like Guokeng. I got off the train and bought a standing ticket to Beijing as there were no seats available when I was not traveling from the starting station of Fuzhou city. At about midnight, I got on the train to Beijing and stood in the middle of the train cabinet as no seat was available. **Summer in Fujian and Zhejiang Provinces was sweltering, with a temperature of about 36 C (97 F). It was much hotter in a train full of passengers with a temperature of more than 40 C.** There was no air conditioner and no fans inside the train in 1980. It was better when the train moved because almost all the windows were open, so winds could blow in. **Like a steam cage, it became worse when the train stopped at stations. Most people on the train were tired, exhausted, sweating, and sleepy in the middle of the night. I needed to stand up against other people as it was so crowded. Getting drinking water and passing this crowd to the toilet room was hard. Some people even occupied toilet rooms as there was hardly any spare room to stand up. After a couple of hours on this train, I felt stomach pain, probably because it was too hot and lack of water. I had no choice and nowhere to complain and get help except to continue standing up, suffering, and** controlling myself. I understood that this was the real life I had to face from then on. **Finally, I got a seat in Hangzhou after more than 12 hours of standing on this train at one o'clock in the afternoon of the 2nd day.** I could then sleep and rest even though it was very hot. The trip on the train was a bit easier after I had a seat. Many people arrived and got off at each major station, like Shanghai, Nanjing, Jinan, and Tianjin. I was curious about those places even though they were inside railway stations. People could get off the train to stretch, get drinking water, and buy food. This long trip lasted three days and two nights from Lindun to Beijing. In Jinan station of Shandong Province, I met a passenger from the local area who spoke a pure Shandong dialect. He was very talkative and spoke to me continuously for a long time even though I could hardly understand him. Finally, the train arrived at Beijing railway station at about 10:00 pm on the 3rd day. **I got off the train and walked out of the station, but I did not see anyone from Tsinghua University to help new students.** I was told later that I arrived one day earlier than their schedule. Before my trip, I probably missed the information passing through so many layers of communication from Tsinghua to my local village headquarters. After asking around, I was told that public buses were still going from Beijing railway station to the Tsinghua campus. **Beijing railway station was located in the southern part of Beijing, while Tsinghua was in the far northern suburb of Beijing. I needed to take three different bus routes across Beijing City to get there. I had no choice but to go before the buses stopped at midnight. The city was dark and almost empty, and few passengers were on the buses at those hours. I kept asking different people on the buses as I feared missing the right stop or getting on the wrong bus. I did not want to wander on the street as a stranger at midnight if I did not get to the Tsinghua campus that night. At about midnight 12:00 am, I arrived at the South Gate of the Tsinghua campus, located at the south border of the campus.**

Tsinghua has a huge campus, which was a royal garden before 1911. I showed my documents to gate guards and was told **that the department dormitory I was admitted into was on the most northern part of campus. It would take more than 45 minutes to walk across the whole Tsinghua campus, as shown on the map of Tsinghua.** Fortunately, one senior student from Henan Province was walking by then. He told me he could show me how to get there as he needed to walk to his dorm, too. **I was exhausted, tired, thirsty, and hungry after more than 60 hours of travel on the road with little sleep, food, and drink. I still needed to carry two heavy, ugly luggage bags at midnight, walking 45 minutes on campus.** The campus was dark and quiet at that time. Finally, I got to the dorm by about 1:00 am. **The dorm guard saw a skinny teenage boy in awkward, dirty, and bad-smelling cloth, obviously from a poor rural area, with two huge bags.** He was nice to let me move into my dorm room after I showed him all the documents. My bulky quilt and the wooden case had arrived in that dorm building before me. I was told that I arrived one day earlier, and few students of the new class were there yet. I went to bed quickly after more than 60 hours on the road. On the morning of the 2nd day, I woke up to purchase some personal items like a hot water container (热水瓶 or thermos) and a washbasin from a nearby small store in Zhaonanyuan.

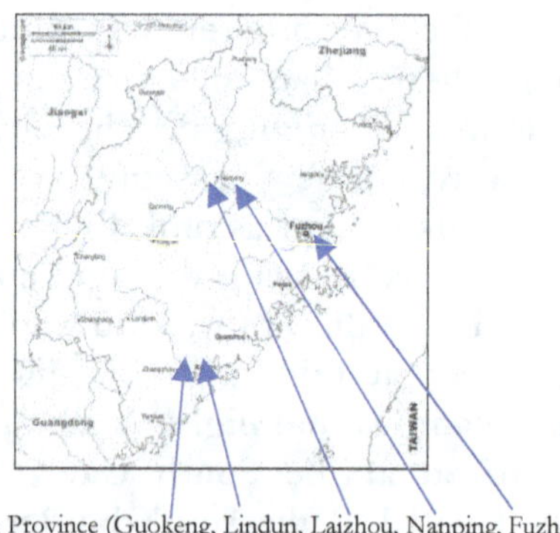

Map of Fujian Province (Guokeng, Lindun, Laizhou, Nanping, Fuzhou)

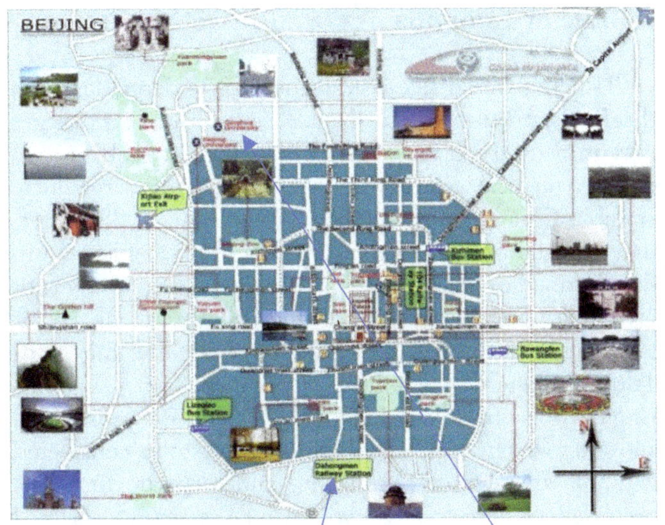

Map of Beijing City (Beijing Train Station and Tsinghua Campus)

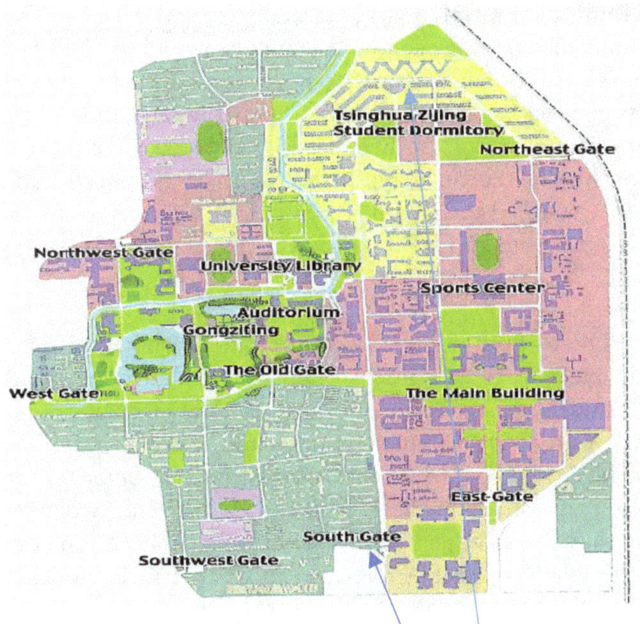

Map of Tsinghua Campus (South Gate, My Dormitory)

7.3 Life in Tsinghua

Tsinghua had a five-year agenda for undergraduates in the 1980s, one more year than almost all four-year colleges except medical schools. At that time, high school students entered medical schools directly for their undergraduate study in China. After five years of study and a BS degree, they became physicians to see patients. I was admitted to the Hydraulic Machinery major in the Department of Hydraulic Engineering. After the 1990s, this major in Hydraulic Machinery was merged into the major of Turbomachinery in the Department of Thermal Engineering. In 1980, high school students were only allowed to list five universities they wanted to be considered without any input of majors and departments they preferred. There were two major categories: STEM (Science, Technology, Engineering, and Math) and liberal arts. In the 2nd year of high school, each student chose STEM or Liberal arts. I naturally picked STEM. The admittance rate was so low that anyone would feel lucky to be selected by any university. The chosen universities would assign you to a major and a department inside their universities based on their needs. Once you were picked, you had to accept or reject the offer. If you rejected the offer, you had to stay one more year in high school to try Gaokao again and apply for new universities the following year.

There were four classes for the freshmen of the Hydraulic Engineering department. Each of them had about 30 students. One class was for Agricultural Hydraulics, and two were for Hydraulic Engineering, which focused on building dams and hydraulic electric power stations. Our class was on hydraulic machinery for building hydraulic turbines and water pumps. All male students in the Hydraulic Engineering department and all male students from the Department of Engineering Physics lived in the 13th dormitory building, which had five floors. Each floor accommodated one grade of male students. There was one big toilet room and one big washroom for all 120 students in each grade on one side of the building for hydraulic engineering. Hot and boiled water was also provided on each floor. The other half of this building was for male students of the Engineering Physics department. The 13th dormitory was located in the northern part of the Tsinghua campus. We could see farming fields outside our building at that time. There were a group of dormitory buildings nearby, including several cafeterias. We were assigned to eat at the No. 4 cafeteria, 10 minutes' walk from our dorm. Classrooms were scattered around the whole campus, though most were close to the main library and the auditorium. In one semester, our class had a Mechanical Design course in the Main Building by the Eastern Gate of Campus from 8:00 am to 9:00 am, and we needed to walk across the campus for more than 45 minutes to attend the course of Chemistry at 10:00 am in a building near northern Gate of campus. At that time, only a few students had a bicycle, which was expensive for college students.

Our class had 26 male students and two female ones. All 26 male students lived in the five rooms on the 5th floor of the 13th dormitory building. There were six students in my room, Room 513. Among them, CY Shen was from Nanchong of Sichuan Province; JW Miao was from Tianjin; FY Xie was from Tiangmeng of Hebei Province; NW Wen was from Nanfang of Hubei Province, and HJ Zhao was from Hechi of Guangxi Province. We had a room of about 16 square meters with three double-layer beds and three tables with six drawers. Everyone could study in the dorm with a tiny table and drawer if they wanted, though most of us chose to study in the classrooms and library. In the 1980s, all students in our class would take the same courses before graduation. The department and the university designed the course agenda. Among 28 students in our class, nine were from rural areas, including CY, FY in our dorm, and HH Zheng from Huian County in Quanzhou City of Fujian

Province.

Tsinghua had a challenging and competitive academic agenda for its students even though it had one more year of college than other four-year universities. Students had a more overwhelming study schedule than those in 4-year colleges. Many universities in China then, including Tsinghua, copied most of the higher educational styles from Soviet Unions, with very detailed major definitions and plans. We had a lot of STEM courses like math, physics, chemistry, and material mechanics for the first two years. The exams were challenging as students were bright and the best from their high schools, counties, or provinces. Most teachers were also graduates from Tsinghua themselves, so they understood the students' backgrounds, including their strengths and weaknesses. There were many excellent teachers like Jiehua Wu in advanced Calculus and Xueyu Zhou in Hydraulics and Fluid Mechanics. The teachers always had one difficult exam question accounting for 10% of the grade, which almost all students could not answer. So, average grades for each class and exam were usually between 70% and 80%. Less than 5% of students had over 90% of the grade. We had to get up early in the morning to do exercises like jogging before breakfast. The classes started at 8:00 am and ended at about 12:00 pm. There was a short lunch break. The afternoon classes started at about 1:30 pm and finished at 5:00 pm. Students were required to have outdoor physical exercise before dinner time at about 6:00 pm. One popular exercise for many Tsinghua students and me was long-distance running. We would run from our dorm to the northern gate of campus, pass Yuanmingyuan, and come back to campus through the northwestern gate before coming to the dorm. **Yuanmingyuan was one of the most significant royal gardens in the world, with a vast collection of invaluable treasuries from royal families of the Qing dynasty between 1600 and 1900. Unfortunately, it was looted and burnt in about 1900 by allied troops of eight foreign countries.** Many treasury items were stolen and are now displayed in major museums in London, Paris, Tokyo, Berlin, New York, and St Petersburg. After dinner, we would go to a classroom or library to study until 9:30 pm and go to bed at about 10:00 pm. Usually, main library seats were fully occupied quickly, the same in most classrooms near the dorms. Sometimes, we needed to look for a classroom seat for a while. The light of the dorm was turned off after 10:00 pm.

7.3.1 Different Climate and Food Challenges

Different Climate: Beijing has quite a different climate from my hometown in Fujian. It is very chilly, even in the fall and spring. The weather is much drier in the fall, and people need to drink much water. There were a lot of sandstorms in the spring of the 1980s. The heating gas was turned on in the winter after November 15th, and the room became much drier. The first year was tough for me to get used to this kind of weather. I trembled a lot in September 1980 during swimming class and had to leave in the middle of class to return to the dorm and put on more clothes to avoid catching a cold. There was no air ventilation in the buildings, and I had breathing difficulty in the classrooms in winter as all windows were closed and sealed. I also did not know how to prepare a quilt well in Beijing, especially during winter. I brought a heavy quit of 5 kg from Changtai, which was too hot most of the time, including winter when there was a heating gas. I gradually learned that the best combination would be two light quilts, which could be used when cold.

Food Challenge

Food was also a challenge for me at that time. There was a minimum of cabbage, white carrot, and potato vegetables during the winter season, while there were fresh vegetables in Changtai during all seasons. We had an allocation on staple food (主食) of 18 kg per month, our primary food source and energy as meat and vegetables were not cheap or reasonably available. **Among them, 4.5 kg was coarse grain (粗粮) like corn, 10.5 kg was wheat flour like buns or noodles, and only 3 kg of rice.** I ate rice every day in Changtai. Usually, I needed a small bowl of porridge for breakfast, which accounted for 1.5 kg of my rice allocation in Beijing monthly. With that, I only had 1.5 kg of rice left to have dried rice each month, which was very hard for me. I never had any coarse-grain food before coming to Beijing. One day in Tsinghua Cafeteria, I saw a bunch of yellow corn cakes, which I thought were tasty, like in Fujian, made of flour, sugar, and egg. **I bought two big pieces and had a big bite to try to enjoy them. It disappointed me greatly, and I could hardly swallow them.** I seldom repurchased it after that. Corn soup in the morning was ok with very salty pickles (咸菜). Tsinghua cafeteria provided deep-fried cake (油饼) every day, which was considered a good food for most students. However, I started to have bumps on my lip after a while of eating this every day, probably because of too much inner heat (上火 起泡).

7.3.2 Poor Finance

Financially, it was a difficult time for my family and me from 1980 to 1983, as SiGe and I were in college. ErGe had a monthly salary of about 40 Yuan by that time. He gave SiGe and me about 10 to 15 Yuan per month, which left him and the rest of our family only about 15 Yuan per month. SanGe did his best to work anywhere, including ErGe's factory, to earn extra cash to help. ErGe's 1st and 2nd children were born during that period, which added more financial stress to our family even though it also brought joy to us. I applied for financial assistance in Tsinghua and received the highest amount at 22 Yuans per month, like most other students from rural areas. Tuition and boarding were free at that time in all public universities in China, which was one of the major reasons the admittance rate was so low. There was no private university in China at that time.

I spent about 15 Yuan per month on food in 1980, so I had about 20 Yuan to buy personal items like clothes, books, travel, and others. More winter clothes were needed in Beijing than in Changtai. I barely wore a shoe in Changtai and ran 100 and 400 meters with a bare foot in physical education classes in high school. I did the same in my first year at Tsinghua, which was quite surprising to most people. 15 Yuan per month in 1980 was enough for food, but this increased yearly due to inflation. It started to feel tight in 1983 when I spent about 35 Yuan per month in Beijing. It worsened from 1984 to 1985 as the cost of living rose significantly compared with 1980. I did my best to save money and did some summer jobs whenever they were available on campus. During that period, student jobs were not quite popular and available, especially for Tsinghua students, as we were located in a remote suburb of Beijing with a vast campus. That was the main reason that I could not afford to go home to visit my family in Changtai from 1983 to 1985. SiGe graduated in the summer of 1983 and worked as a teacher at Jiangxi Wuyan Tea School, a two-year college. ErGe asked him to start giving me 15 Yuan per month so ErGe could focus on supporting the growing family with his limited salary. In addition, ErGe and SanGe parted from us in 1984 after SanGe got married and had his first kid. With that, each brother was on their own, leading their own families, which is a tradition in China. Mom spent most of her time with SanGe in Lindun. **Before my graduation in 1985, I had never eaten in an external restaurant during my five-year stay in Beijing.** It cost much more in an outer restaurant than in a non-profit campus cafeteria. On graduation day, our roommates decided to have a farewell meal in Quanjude for Beijing roasted duck. That was also the first time I tasted Beijing roasted duck and the only time I had a meal in an external restaurant in Beijing before 1985.

7.3.3 Only Visiting Home Twice in Five Years

Due to financial stress, I spent the next five Chinese New Year's on the Tsinghua campus alone and only went home twice during my five-year study in Tsinghua from 1980 to 1985. Chinese New Year, called the Spring Festival, is the most important holiday in China. All family members will do their best to reunite on this day, similar to Thanksgiving and Christmas in the USA. The first time I visited home was in the summer of 1981, and 2nd time was in the summer of 1983. The first Chinese New Year in 1980 was very hard for me as it was too far away and expensive to go home. Tsinghua University organized a Chinese New Year dinner for students who were on campus. Some teachers came to have dinner with us in the No. 4 cafeteria. The dinner was done by about 7:00 pm. I returned to the dorm and read a book for a while before going to bed by about 10:00 pm. My roommate JW was nice to invite me to spend the spring festival at his home in Tianjin. I hesitated and did not go eventually, primarily due to a tight budget. I had to live on whatever I had each month financially, and any extra spending might put me in a difficult position like what occurred later in 1984 during the field trip to Hangzhou. HJ Zhao and GW Wei from Guangxi Province also did not go home because it was too far away. We three visited the Great Wall on Chinese New Year and took a picture together in the Great Wall. My mother was sad that I could not go home for the Spring Festival and refused to sit with other family members to have dinner on Chinese New Year's Eve during those five years. I learned this in the Chinese New Year of 1985 and finally saw my mother sitting together with others for dinner on that Chinese New Year's Eve.

7.3.4 Awkward Experience During On-Site Training Trip

In 1984, our class went to the Xiaoshan Hydraulic

Turbine factory in Hangzhou of Zhejiang Province for a site class that lasted several months. We were also arranged to tour Xinanjiang (新安江) and Fuchunjiang (富春江) hydraulic power stations. Soldiers guarded the Xinanjiang hydraulic power station because of their strategic location and dam size. Its dam formed Qiandaohu (千岛湖), a popular tourist site in China. We also got to visit the site of Yanziling Diaoyutai (严子陵钓鱼台).

More expenses occurred during this field trip, which put me in a tough financial situation as I did not have extra funding. We lived in dorms provided by the factory. Most students decided to tour nearby cities on weekends before leaving Xiaoshan. I visited Hangzhou with almost all my classmates over the weekend by public bus, which cost me all the remaining money I had. The following weekend, our roommates wanted to visit Shaoxing, a well-known ancient city in China. I had to decline their invitation and stay in the factory dorm alone because I ran out of money. I just told them I did not feel well and could not go. We had to change trains in Shanghai while returning to Beijing. Most students would stay there for one or two days to visit this biggest and the most prosperous city in China. Students were self-organized into different small groups for the touring. Our small group walked around several main streets in Shanghai, such as Nanjing and Huaihai roads. We had lunch in a tiny restaurant by the street during lunchtime and ordered several dishes together. **I could not afford to pay for the lunch as I had no money and needed to wait for next month's money from SiGe and the university. That was one of the most embarrassing moments of my life**. One of our classmates paid for my lunch. It was the first time I had eaten in a restaurant with others, and I was responsible for paying my share. I did not handle it well, as I lacked experience. I should have indicated that I would repay him when I received the next month's money from SiGe and the university. I am still grateful to this classmate whenever I think of that moment.

7.3.5 Friends and Valuable Friendship

One evening in the spring of 1981, near the No. 4 cafeteria, I heard a familiar Mingnan dialect conversation, which I had not heard since I arrived in Tsinghua. I turned around and saw two students and bravely asked them if they were from the South Fujian area. It turned out that both were from Longhai District, which is also part of Zhangzhou City, such as Changtai. Longhai is a neighboring district of Changtai and is also located between Zhangzhou and Xiamen. One of the students was CZ Guo, and another was PW Liu. CZ was from Shima, and PW was from Jiaomei. They happened to be in the same grade as mine and attended Tsinghua in 1980. ZC was in the Department of Thermal Engineering, majoring in HVAC (Heating, Ventilation, and Air Conditioning). PW was in the Department of Engineering Physics and lived in the same 13th dormitory building as mine. From that moment, I was invited to join their activities after school. Longhai had many more college students in Beijing because it was a bigger district than Changtai in the 1980s in terms of population and area. I was quickly introduced to PH Huang, who was also from Longhai. He was in the Mechanical Engineering Department at Tsinghua. We became lifetime friends and are all in the USA now. We played a lot of card games during breaks, sometimes overnight. We also ate together a lot in the cafeteria. None of us barely knew how to cook even a simple noodle soup. Students sometimes cooked simple food like ramen in dorms with a small electric oven, which was officially prohibited. Whoever was caught might be in trouble. The cooking utensils would be confiscated.

More friends were involved in our group later in 1981, including WY Yang from Shima of Longhai District in Beijing Agricultural Machinery University, JH Huang from Shima of Longhai, and MD Liang from Changtai. JH and MD were at Beijing Physical Educational University. In

1983, TH Huang and LW Liu from Longhai were admitted to Tsinghua. TH Huang was the younger brother of PH Huang. LW Liu was the younger brother of PW Liu. Our group became bigger. HD Huang, the sister of PH Huang and TH Huang, also joined the group sometime in 1985. In addition to this group, FC Shen and ZY Shen from Changtai attended Beijing Agricultural Machinery University and Beijing Jiaotong University in 1981. MS Chai from Changtai attended Beijing Foreign Language University in 1984. From MS, I got to know another hometown senior, YW Liang, from Jiangdu of Lindun. YW graduated from a university in the 1960s and worked in Beijing afterward. FH Yuan and ZZ Zeng from Zhangzhou City were in Tsinghua's Department of Engineering Mechanics. We got to talk and met often in the same classes and other locations. In the summer of 1983, I went back home with FH Yuan.

These college students from my hometown areas got to see each other often during the breaks. I was not so lonely at that time. PH Huang had a better family background economically than most of us, especially me, and did cover a lot of food for us. I appreciated his generosity a lot. I did visit Shima in the summer of 1983 and stayed at PH's home. PH's whole family was very nice and hospitable during my visit. PH, CZ, and WY Yang got together and had a good time in Shima. We also visited Xiamen, which was my first time. I saw a different and better lifestyle in a port town near the ocean and realized how poor Lindun and my family were. PH Huang, CZ Guo, and PW Liu also visited me in Lindun that summer at my invitation. We took a hot spring shower in Lindun and went swimming in the river by my home in the evening. The water in the river was crystal clear, and we could see fish swimming as there was no pollution in this mountainous area. I felt sorry that we had to sleep in a neighboring peasant's home because there were not enough beds and rooms for guests to sleep in. There was only one bedroom, 16 square meters, and one storage room for my family. The food my family could come up with was also simple and primitive. From that time, I started to be very careful about inviting friends' homes as we lacked the basic conditions to accommodate them. After the visit, they were amazed at how poor my family was and how I grew up to attend Tsinghua after all those years.

The valuable friendships I enjoyed in Beijing helped me a lot, including overcoming loneliness during the holiday seasons of Chinese New Year and summer breaks.

7.3.6 Poor Health

I had poor health in Beijing during my study in Tsinghua, probably from poor nutrition, unknown hepatitis B virus, bad climate, and unfamiliar food types. I frequently caught colds and fevers. I had been sweating so much that my mat (褥子) wetted often and eventually got rotten. One day, I got very sick and had to walk slowly for more than 45 minutes to the university clinic, which was quite far from my dorm. **The doctor told me I had a fever of 39.2 C (more than 102.6 F)** and prescribed me some medicines. I told him I had no appetite and was given a patient meal order from the doctor. When I went to the cafeteria and handled that patient's meal order, the cook told me they were too busy to prepare meals for all the students and could only give me a simple noodle soup. It was a soup with noodles, a few pieces of vegetables, oil, and salt. **That noodle soup with a few pieces of vegetables (or so-called 阳春面 or 清汤面) tasted so good to me at that time**. However, I did not bother the cook again, even though it was just a simple warm noodle soup with vegetables, as I did not want to see their cold faces. Instead, I just drank a lot of hot water with some crackers until I recovered to the extent of eating regular food like other students. Drinking a lot of hot water made me sweat more and reduced the fever. It also got my clothes and cot wet too. I could switch clothes, but not a cot, as that was my only one. My roommate JW generously offered me some oranges during my sickness. Orange was considered a luxurious food for college students then, especially in northern China, like Beijing. I also started eating spicy food during that 5-year stay at Tsinghua as it helped me sweat more and feel better. Those spicy foods gradually damaged my stomach as my stomach had not been used to this kind of food since childhood. **I got sick with a fever so often and sweated so much that my mat was almost rotten when I graduated in 1985**. I weighed less than 50 kg in 1985, with a height of 1.70 m at 20 when I graduated.

7.3.7 Reading and Other Skills

Extensive Reading: I had no spare book to read in Lindun and Changtai before 1980. Extra books besides textbooks were expensive and considered a luxury for a peasant family like us. I was amazed at the number of books in the Tsinghua library and started reading a lot during winter and summer breaks. I could not go home during the first winter break of the Chinese New Year period in 1980 because it cost too much to travel. I checked out many books from the library and read in crazy ways of day and night, often several hours continuously. I was pretty much alone during that year's winter break, with no friends except several classmates who stayed on campus. I started with Chinese history from the Qin dynasty, the first emperor of China, about 2000 years ago, to the last Qing dynasty. Each dynasty has 2 to 3 books to cover. It took 2 to 3 years, in several winter and summer breaks, for me to finish reading those books on Chinese history. In addition, I read many well-known novels that were translated into Chinese versions, like "The Bible", "The Red and the Black" by Stendhal, "Les Miserable" by Victor Hugo, "War and Peace" and "Anna Karenina" by Leo Tolstoy et al. I was fascinated by "Three Kingdoms" (三国演义) and "Water Margin" (水浒传) and bored with "Dream of the Red Chamber" (红楼梦), "Strange Tales from a Chinese Studio" (

聊斋), and "Das Kapital" (资本论). Most content in political economics classes taught in high school, and Tsinghua was from the book "Das Kapital." After many years in the USA, I realized that what Marx described was still partially true regarding capitalism in Western countries. I was too young to fully understand many features and characters in those novels and books. However, they did provide insights into different cultures and countries. I was hungry and curious to explore those new worlds and other cultures in those books, which might have led me to move and drift for many years in different places. As a poor student, I read those books full of imagination like a sponge absorbing water.

Bridge: Bridge became popular in Tsinghua in 1980. I attended several seminars by well-known players. Our roommates started playing bridge in 1981 almost every Saturday night. JW Miao partnered with LW Wen, and CY Shen did with me. We also attended some local tournaments on the Tsinghua campus. I enjoyed this game a lot. It was much more sophisticated than the 40-point game I played in childhood. Bridge requires good cooperation between you and your partner during the bidding stage to reach the optimal deal based on your card situation, your partner's, and your opponents'. You also need to forecast and predict the card distribution of your opponent well in each round to win. Usually, a good bridge player can predict which cards your opponents have after 3 to 4 rounds of cards.CY and I worked well together as partners. I continued paying bridges in graduate studies in Shanghai and had QZ Pan as a partner from SJTU (Shanghai Jiaotong University). In 1987, we won a championship in a major tournament in Shanghai among hundreds of selected competitors representing many research and design institutes. However, I slowly cut back on participating in a bridge competition afterward because most players were heavy smokers. The bad air quality in the room made me sick with an intense headache.

Computer Programming: I started BASIC programming in 1981 in a class and was fascinated by it. We needed to punch a card to input lines of codes. In 1982, I took FORTRAN and liked it a lot. Tsinghua required each undergraduate to have a BS graduation research project and a thesis done in the fifth year before you could graduate. That was equivalent to the requirements of an MS degree graduate in most universities in China and the USA. I chose "Finite Element Fluid Flow Analysis on Hydraulic Turbine" and worked with a group of teachers and classmates. The theory part was done and provided by Professor CR Lin, based on the three-dimensional streamline theory. Dr. Wu Zhonghua developed this theory while he was doing his Ph.D. at MIT (Massachusetts Institute of Technology) in the 1940s. It was widely used in the development of turbomachinery worldwide, including turbines used in aerospace. Dr. Wu Zhonghua was the director of the Thermal Physics Institute at the Chinese Academy of Science in the 1980s. In our graduation project, I needed to first review and understand the theory part from Professor CR Lin. Then, I needed to program the simulation into FORTRAN code and make it work. I enjoyed and did an excellent job in my BS thesis project, laying a good foundation for my future career, including an MS in Shanghai and a Ph.D. study in the USA. Our project team got a chance to visit Harbin Hydraulic and Electric Motor Corporation in Heilongjiang Province, the largest of its kind in China and probably one of the biggest in the world at that time. We also visited the Shenyang Pump Factory in Liaoning Province during that trip. It was the spring of 1985, which was very dry. A big fire before our visit burnt down a significant portion of Harbin City, as many buildings were built of wood. Therefore, we could only eat cold food in Harbin during our visit because no resident was allowed to cook themselves to minimize potential fire breaks.

7.3.8 Where to Go After Graduation

This was a big decision for us. Most of the students in my class chose to go to graduate study like me. Based on my GPA ranking, positive feedback, and encouragement from professors in my major of Hydraulic Machinery, I had a good chance to continue my graduate study at Tsinghua if I chose to. I hesitated for a while and decided to go to Shanghai to continue my graduate study at MA Institute of China and SJTU based on the following factors: (a) The market future of hydraulic machinery was not promising. Technology had existed for a long time, and no breakthrough was expected in this industry. This was the primary reason most of our classmates eventually chose different fields. Only about 20% stay in this field now. Several years later, after my graduation, Tsinghua merged this major into more general Turbomachinery in the Thermal Engineering Department, which was the right thing to do. (b) Location of the city: Beijing was a tough city for me because of its climate and food. Shanghai would be better for my health and much closer to home in Changtai. I missed spending time with my family during Chinese New Year in the last five years. (c) The marketing future of marine and naval architecture was much brighter and exciting to me, which turned out to be true many years later.

I successfully studied in Tsinghua and enjoyed five years of study and friendships there with my classmates, roommates, teachers, and friends. I learned a lot and got rigorous training on my character and capacity to succeed in harsh conditions. My only regret was that I was too young to attend university at 15. Though I was competitive and doing well academically in Tsinghua, my young body and mind were still growing and not mature enough to perform better otherwise in this highly competitive environment. At that time, I was too young to understand the real world's dedicated social and personal relations, which were also quite different between north and south, rural and city areas in China. That was one of the reasons I asked my daughter in 2014 not to rush to finish her undergraduate studies, even though she could get it done in two years.

Tsinghua Graduation Classmates of HM80 July 1985 (Walter at 3rd From Left on Last Row)

The above graduation class photos were taken in front of the auditorium before we departed the Tsinghua campus in July 1985. I was third from left on the last row. We were pretty close after five years of living in the same dorm building and taking the same classes in the same classrooms. This was especially true for those living in the same room and those from the same province. We were ambitious after five years of intensive training in Tsinghua. Most of us went to graduate study in different universities and academic research institutes. Only a few of us stayed in the field of hydraulic machinery as the job market was not very good then. After I was admitted to the graduate study program at MA and SJTU, my classmate BG Meng decided to join MA to work over there. We two would become much closer in the next seven years in Shanghai before I headed to the USA for my Ph.D. study in 1992. MC Zhang, in our class, also went to SJTU for his graduate study in 1985.

Chapter 8
The Trip Back to Changtai in July 1985 After Graduation from Tsinghua

Visit to MA I visited the MA Institute of China in Shanghai, where I would go for my graduate study on my way back to Fujian after graduation. I stayed in the dormitory of SJTU during the trip with a friend, CB Xiao. CB was one grade below me from Changtai No. 1 High School and attended SJTU in 1981. He graduated in 1985 because SJTU was a 4-year college at that time. He also entered graduate study in 1985 at SJTU. I contacted him ahead of time and was able to stay in his dormitory to save on the cost of a motel during my visit to MA. It was my first time meeting him, and we quickly became good friends. Unfortunately, he passed away in 1993 when I was in the US, which was sudden and sad for me. MA had several locations, with one main campus on Gaoxiong Road close to South Xizang Road. I got to see my advisor, S. Zheng, and his colleagues. He invited me to dinner that day, so I met his family, too. **That was the first time I had dinner at other people's homes in Beijing and Shanghai since I left Changtai in 1980.**

Visit to Wuyuan (婺源县, Jiangxi Province) I visited SiGe on my way home from Shanghai. Wuyuan in Jiangxi Province was about a 5-hour bus drive from Quzhou (衢州市) railway station in Zhejiang Province. There is a big mountain between them. I needed to stay in Quzhou for one night and took the public bus to Wuyuan County Township the next morning. The road was mostly over the big mountain, and road conditions were bad. After arriving at the bus station in WuYuan, it was too late to catch another bus to SiGe's school in a nearby village about 5 km away. I had to stay in a motel overnight. At that time, we communicated by letter as public phones were unpopular. After checking into a motel, I went to the post office late in the afternoon and tried to call SiGe. I could not find SiGe over the phone and could only leave a message for him. The voice quality of the phone was so bad that I could barely understand what the other person said. SiGe later told me that he and another colleague had ridden a bike to the town that evening and had failed to find me in any motel. I took an early morning bus for 15 minutes on the 2nd day and showed up surprisingly in front of SiGe on his college campus. I had to walk alone with all my luggage on a muddy road in a rural area for 30 minutes before getting to the campus. The campus was in a small village full of tea trees in the nearby hills.

It was the first time I met SiGe's girlfriend, MS Shen. She was a student of SiGe at Tea College and looked very young. We visited her family in a remote village near Jiangwan town, about 25 km away. The village was tiny, with probably 100 people, and was located by a river. The place was beautiful, and many scenes in the movie "Shining Red Star" (闪闪的红星) were taken over there in the 1970s. The village is very close to Yellow Mountain, a national park of China and a world heritage site. Wuyuan was part of Anhui Province and is now a popular tourist site in China. It was also the first time SiGe visited MS's family. MS's parents and family were friendly and welcoming. We swam in the river in the evening and ate delicious local food like FenZhengRou (steamed pork belly) and spicy pepper. The area was still poor, like Lindun, but the people and neighborhood were friendly. I had a good time over there.

Boarding a Public Bus That Almost Fell into a Deep Cliff on the Way Back to Lindun

SiGe gave me 37 Yuan, all he had before I returned to QuZhou railway station. I had run out of money at that time. I needed to take a public bus for another 5-hour drive over that dangerous mountain road. The public bus was packed with about 50 people. Most of them were local peasants. **On the way downhill, I heard a big explosion, and the whole bus swung over to the cliff's edge. The bus's tire hit something and burst, and the entire bus almost lost balance and rolled over the mountain valley hundreds of meters deep. Most passengers would have lost their lives if that happened**. Fortunately, the driver was skillful in steering the bus away to the inner and safe area and gradually slid the bus to a safe and broader area. Many passengers were very scared and slowly calmed down after a long silence. I was too young to think through what could mean to a life at that time. The driver changed the tire quickly before we slowly descended the hill by the road. I probably would not dare to drive or sit in any car or a bus now on that kind of mountain road. It was like the notorious death road in Ecuador, South America.

Visit to Xiamen After leaving Wuyan, I went directly to Xiamen to visit MJ Yang. MJ was also a graduate of Changtai No. 1 High School in 1981, like CB Xiao. He attended Xiamen University in 1981. MJ had a training class at Bejing Reming University in the spring of 1985 and visited me in Tsinghua before my graduation. His family moved from Changtai to Xiamen several years ago. It was the first time I stayed in Xiamen City overnight at a friend's home, and I got a good chance to tour Xiamen University and Xiamen City with MJ.

Chapter 9
Graduate Study in Shanghai from 1985 to 1988

I started my graduate study for a Master's degree in September 1985. It was arranged that all academic courses in the first year would be taken at SJTU (Shanghai Jiaotong University), and the MS thesis research would be done at the MA Institute of China for the rest of the one-and-a-half years. MA had several major locations, as shown in the attached map of Shanghai. Its headquarters was on East Nanjing Road, close to North Sichuan Road, five minutes from Waitan. Major office buildings and lab facilities were on Gaoxiong Road near South Xizang Road. There was one division on Yuanmingyuan Road near East Beijing Road, which is also five minutes from Waitan. MA had a major residential area for its employees on Longchang Road in Yanpu District, which was in northeastern Shanghai. New graduate students were arranged to live in a dorm at that location for the first semester and had to travel to SJTU to attend classes every day. SJTU is located in Xuhui District at the corner of Guangyuan Road and Huashan Road in southwestern Shanghai. **I needed to get up at about 5:30 am and take three public buses to travel across Shanghai City. After arriving at SJTU's campus, I would have a simple breakfast in the campus cafeteria before 8:00 am for the class. It was painful and disappointing as I spent more than four hours on the buses daily.** Fortunately, MA adjusted the policy during 2nd semester to let us live in a dorm at its campus on South Xizang Road. It took only 30 minutes to bike to the SJTU campus from that location. One year later, MA and SJTU arranged to have all new graduate students from MA live in SJTU's dorm in the first year of course study. This was much more convenient for those new graduate students.

Because I was in the Naval Architecture and Shipbuilding industry, my class at SJTU was with the Department of Naval Architecture and Ocean Engineering. I had to spend a lot of time catching up with new knowledge in this industry.

Map of Shanghai (SJTU, MA at Xizang Road, Nanjing Road, and Longchang Road)

Dormitory at Gaoxiong Road (1987)

When I first arrived in Shanghai in 1985, many classmates and roommates were surprised to see me so skinny and malnourished. **I probably looked more like a refugee from a developing country then. Some friends later sincerely asked me if most students at Tsinghua University looked like me. I replied, "No, I am exceptional on campus."** Life in Shanghai was easier than in Beijing. As a graduate student, I received a monthly stipend of about 50 yuan. MA also paid tuition and boarding for graduate study. The climate and food were better for me as it was close to my hometown of Changtai. There were more vegetables, and the food prices were lower than in Beijing. I started to have a normal life like most graduate students. I could even save some money to help my family, especially during the Chinese New Year period when I was back in Lindun. I started to gain weight gradually over the next several years, and my health improved, too.

9.1 Trip to Qingdao in Shandong Province

One advantage of doing MS thesis research in MA was that there were many realistic and challenging projects coming from the industry. I was first asked to get to know customers and the industry to visit customer sites and understand their needs and challenges. After finishing all my SJTU courses, I got a chance to visit Qingdao at the end of 1986 because MA just delivered a newly designed vessel for the shallow ocean area in the Shengli oil field. That vessel introduced a new patented technology using a water jet propulsion assembly, which allowed it to sail on a very shallow ocean area near the coast with great maneuverability. The test sail of this new vessel was in the Yellow Sea near Qingdao. I observed the first ocean trial sail of this unique vessel and helped take some valuable photos, which were used in later patent applications. It was the first time I boarded a ship in the ocean and experienced a massive swing of the whole boat when there was a big wind. Fortunately, I did not experience any seasickness. There was a celebration and a banquet after the meeting. It was the first time I tasted well-known Qingdao beer and delicious seafood from that area.

9.2 Trip to Jiamusi in Heilongjiang Province

My MS thesis research would be on water jet propulsion using a pump assembly, mostly used in fast-speed boats. I was asked to visit one of the major customers. The border troops near Russia, or the Soviet Union before 1990, used the speed boats with water jet propulsion designed by MA. We boarded a train from Shanghai to Harbin in northeastern China first, then stayed in a hostel at Harbin Shipbuilding University (船舶工程学院) for one night. The hostel was in one massive building built in the Soviet Union style. Armed guards were at the front of the university to check our identification. On the 2nd day, we took another train to Jiamusi, located further northeast of Harbin. Someone from a border troop picked us up from the railway station and sent us to their base near the border of China and Russia. The base was in a pretty remote area with farmers and small hills nearby. We stayed in their base for the next several days, sleeping in their hostel rooms like those soldiers. It was in the early summer of 1987 (May), and I felt quite chilly over there compared to Shanghai. The early morning of the 2nd day, one young soldier of about 18 years old brought us breakfast, which included bunches of steam buns and cooked warm milk in a big washbasin (脸盆). **That was the first time in my life I drank milk.** The milk was fresh from cows raised nearby. It smelt and tasted so good that I still thought it was the best milk I had ever had, even after so many years in the USA. I got to board the fast-speed boat on the river that was the border between Russia and China. At that time, the relationship between China and Russia was not warm, so border troops from both sides were not friendly. The river could be pretty shallow. Soldiers needed a boat that could go faster than Russia's counterpart. Both sides frequently raced in the same river to show their strength. There was a test drive of a new boat first, then an evaluation by experts from this field to see if the ship met all requirements. At the end of the visit, the boat successfully passed all tests. A big celebration and a banquet were held. It was the first time I tasted many well-known dishes in Northeastern China, including fishes of Damaha (大马哈鱼) and Xiaomaha (小马哈鱼) from the Songhua River and organic chicken with organic mushroom from a nearby mountain. On the way back to Shanghai after visiting border troops, I stayed at the home of a colleague's relative in Jiamusi for one night. The family's ancestor, like grandparents, was from Shandong Province in the early 1900s during the period of ChuangGuanDon (闯关东). **It was the first time and the only time I slept in a bed called Kang (炕), popular in the cold northern part of China.** A hole beneath the Kang was linked to the kitchen so the fire smoke could warm up the bed during the wintertime. Like many people from northeastern China, the family was very friendly and hospitable to me.

9.3 Trip to Guangzhou and Guangning Water Pump Factory

My MS thesis research involved a new design method for a water jet pump. New pump prototypes were built in the Guangning water pump factory after developing the theory part and designing several new pumps. I traveled with my thesis deputy advisor, LD Wen, to that factory in 1987. We first took a train from Shanghai to Guangzhou and stayed at a factory hostel for one night. The hostel was a three-bedroom apartment rented by the Guangning Water Pump factory in Guangzhou, with several double beds in each room. On the 2nd day, we boarded a car from the factory and headed for Guangning. Guangning water pump factory was located in Guangning County township in Guangdong Province. It was in the northwestern part of Guangzhou. It took 5 to 6 hours to drive from Guangzhou to Guangning at that time. We needed to go through

Shangshui and Shihui counties before reaching Guangning. The road conditions were poor. There were frequent traffic jams from Guangning County back to Guangzhou, which could easily delay our travel by several hours. Guangning County township was very small, similar to Lindun, but with a larger population. I started tasting delicious food in Guangdong, like Changfen (肠粉), fresh steamed fish, and snakes. The plant manager of this factory, XQ Chen, was a good businessman. He convinced MA to establish this factory as the designated pump supplier for all water jet pumps used in fast-speed boats designed by MA, bringing stable revenue to this remote factory. We were treated well as guests. It was the first time I visited Guangdong Province, which was impressive in its vivid economic activities as it was close to Hong Kong. People there were much more open than in other parts of China.

9.4 Experimental Study of New Pump Design in Hangzhou

In 1987, I needed to conduct an experiment to verify the design, including measuring fluid flow distribution inside pumps. The experiment was done at Zhejiang Mechanical and Scientific Research Institute in Hangzhou, which had a certified pump testing facility. This institute was located in downtown Hangzhou city. It was close to Laodong Road and Hefang Street, about a 5-minute walk from Orioles Singing in the Willows (LiuLangWenYing 柳浪闻莺) in the well-known West Lake (西湖). I spent several months there that year to conduct this experimental study, from designing the testing device for measuring detailed three-dimensional flows inside the pump using a pilot sphere to assembling and finalizing measurements. The pilot sphere was purchased from Tsinghua University as Professor CR Lin's group was doing similar measurements in their research. They had developed this new kind of device. I returned to the Tsinghua campus to purchase the prototype and saw old classmates like CY and others.

Back in Hangzhou, I had several helpers from MA and the Guangning water pump factory. BG Meng and YL were from MA. Two young workers from the Guangning water pump factory were sent because they wanted to be trained as certified pump testing technicians. As mentioned before, my Tsinghua classmate BG joined MA in 1985 after learning I would be there for my graduate studies. We were lucky to be in the same division and group in MA and became much closer than ever. YL was a young technician from the group, mainly helping with testing. Most of the time, we had meals in the institute's cafeteria. Sometimes, we would go out to eat. The meat bun (肉包子) from a vendor on the nearby street was good for breakfast. In the evening, we would go to a small restaurant to order several low-cost dishes by bringing our cheap alcoholic drinks. The meals cost about 10 yuan for five people, which was acceptable as we all got daily meal subsidies. **After more than 8 hours of working, we were hungry and would finish every dish before the next one was delivered**. We also got to tour the West Lake and Hangzhou areas during the weekend. That was a good period of life for me and four other happy bachelors, even though we constantly worked very hard.

9.5 Master Thesis defense

I stayed in Shanghai during the Spring Festival of 1988, Chinese New Year, because I needed to concentrate on working on the thesis before the defense in May 1988.I had dinner at the home of Teacher Zheng in the Chinese New Year's Eye. My classmate MS Fan invited me to his home on Chinese New Year's Day. His family was very hospitable. MS was the 2nd generation in Shanghai, as his parents came from Jiangsu Province. I had a successful graduate defense and graduated on time in May 1988. My MS thesis defense committee included BZ Chen and ZP Qin. Professor Chen was vice president of SJTU. ZP Qin was the Deputy Chief

Engineer of MA and the primary founder of water-jet propulsion technology in China. The Chief Engineer of the Shanghai water pump factory was also on my defense committee.

After graduation, I took a short trip to visit Wuyuan in Jiangxi Province. My mother was with SiGe to help care for his newborn son. Mother was happy over there for almost one year before I brought her home to Lindun during that trip. During that trip, one colleague and friend of SiGe sincerely told me I needed to gain weight and improve my health in order to find a better wife.

9.6 Teacher S Zheng

As my MS thesis advisor, teacher S. Zheng has been one of my life's most important people (贵人) since I left Lindun in 1978. He helped me a lot in my career and personal life. In addition, he was a good person with an excellent technical background and a good personality, like many well-educated people in China at that time. He graduated from Tongji University and joined MA in 1950 with a strong German-style engineering education. Teacher Zheng was a nationally recognized expert on naval architecture devices and water jet propulsion design and development. His father was a general under Liu Xian (刘湘) in Sichuan and lost his life before 1940's. He had an older brother who escaped to Taiwan in 1949 and was a general later under the Nationalist government there. Due to his family background, Teacher Zheng was badly treated during the Cultural Revolution. He later forgave and worked well with people who mistreated him during the Cultural Revolution. I grew up without a father and had been wondering how my father would be if he lived much longer. **Teacher Zheng reminded me a lot of what a father could do to a son: helping, supporting, guiding, encouraging, and understanding**. He invited me to his home for dinner on almost every major holiday since 1985. I have been and will be grateful forever for the kindness and help from him and his whole family during my stay in Shanghai.

9.7 Classmates and Roommates

I had good classmates and roommates in Shanghai. For almost two years, MW Zhang, QZ Pan, CX Liang, and I lived in an apartment on Gaoxiong Road by the main campus of MA. YQ Qin, XG Zhang, and MW Wang lived at their home in Shanghai even though they had been given a bed in that apartment. MW Zhang and I were roommates and became good friends. He invited me to have a nice dinner at his home before he left for the Netherlands to be a visiting scholar. QZ Pan was my partner in the bridge tournament. We played a lot, representing MA in tournaments, and were champion in a major tournament by beating some well-known players in Shanghai. YQ Qin and QZ Pan had invited me and other graduate classmates to have a nice dinner in their apartment right after their wedding. In 1988, we moved to a larger building with more rooms for graduate students and new hires to MA. The building was located on the same main campus as MA on Gaoxiong Road. XG Zhang joined at that time to become a new roommate of mine together with MW Wang until 1992. Many new hires and colleagues lived in that building, including JY Cai. QZ Liang and BG Meng were given a bed in that building, too, though they mostly lived in the office as the dorm was far away from their office on Yuanmingyuan Road.

At that time, Shanghai was notorious for its limited living space. It was common for a family with four people to live in a 12-square-meter room without running water and sewage. Our dorm was behind a pretty noisy factory. The internal living conditions were primitive, with publicly shared bathrooms and washrooms like the university dormitory.

MA Classmates and Teachers (1988, Walter at 5th 2nd row From Left)

9.8 First Real Vacation

In the summer of 1986, I had the first vacation in my life with other graduate classmates, including MW Zhang, YQ Qin, QZ Pan, XG Zhang, and MW Wang. MA provided a small number of activity funds to its graduates each year, and we were allowed to use it to have a field trip we chose. In the summer of 1986, we first took a train to visit Longfu Mountain (龙虎山) in Yingtan of Jiangxi Province. Then we visited Wuyi Mountain (武夷山) of Fujian Province by taking a public bus for several hours from Yingtan. After staying there for two nights, we took buses to visit Sangqing Mountain (三清山) in Jiangxi Province. Over there, we hired a local farmer as a guide to climb up a mountain outside the tourist route. We needed to pass through thick forests without any trail for human beings. My friends were surprised when I climbed much faster and easier than all of them and acted like another guide for the group. They did not know that I grew up on Lindun's mountain and had climbed those mountains routinely before 1980. It was a long trip that lasted more than a week.

In the summer of 1987, this same group visited Mo Gang Mountain in Zhejiang Province. Mo Gang Mountain had several mansions used by Nationalist Government senior officials, including Jiang Jieshi (蒋介石), as their summer vacation homes before 1949.

As students, we were pretty frugal by staying in the lowest-cost motels and eating simple food, as funds from MA could not cover all our travel expenses. **In Sangqing Mountain, we stayed in a hotel built from a cave, which could accommodate about 50 people in a single cave hall. That cave housed a series of simple beds for all boys and girls (男女通铺).** To save money, we had a long argument with the local town government officials in the Wuyi mountain area about switching to a better deal motel booked within hours.

Chapter 10
Engineer Life in Shanghai from 1988 to 1991

10.1 Trip to Zhejiang

In the fall of 1988, after officially joining MA, I had a business trip with several colleagues from MA to tour several major cities in Zhejiang Province. The Zhejiang Transportation Department organized the trip, with stops at Hangzhou, Ningbo, Zhoushan, Taizhou, and Wenzhou. We were well received by the local port officials under the Zhejiang Transportation Department. Besides lunch and dinner, they even sent a host to have meals with us for breakfast. We were treated with all kinds of expensive seafood from those areas. Alcoholic drinks were popular to show their hospitality. They even want to have alcoholic beverages for breakfast with us. That was the first time I had a good understanding of the overall economic development in Zhejiang coastal areas. Those areas are well developed now.

10.2 Design and Manufacturing Engineer in Guangning Water Pump Factory

From February to June 1989, I worked as a supporting design and manufacturing engineer at the Guangning Water Pump factory for MA's new product to be made over there. This was the trip that dramatically improved my health. It also changed my view and plan for my future career. As a guest engineer from MA, the factory received me well, and I had free meals in their cafeteria every day. The cafeteria was also open to external customers and served its employees. They had a simple menu to offer to internal and external customers. **For the first time, I could eat enough**

healthy food without worrying about the cost. I had more protein-rich food than usual because it was free and delicious. I probably had twice the amount of food in the breakfast, including Changfen, porridge with fish, or meat. I was also invited to the most official dinners whenever customers visited this factory. There could be multiple times per week. During this period, I tasted almost all the delicious foods in Guangdong. They were all kinds of fresh steamed fish, snake chicken soup (龙虎斗), expensive soft-shelled turtles (甲鱼), and dim sum breakfast with shrimp dumplings, steamed port ribs, chicken feet, etc. Of course, they also served a lot of fresh vegetables like in Changtai every day. At the same time, I lived a regular and peaceful life in that remote town. I started working at 8:00 am, got off at 5:00 pm Monday to Friday, and rested on Saturday and Sunday. This healthy lifestyle of nutritional food with good rest was the best for my health. By the end of June 1989, when I returned to Shanghai, almost everyone was surprised that I looked much healthier than before. I gained more than five kg of weight in those four months. **For the first time in my life, I reached the milestone of 60 kg in weight at 1.70 m height, which should be expected for most young people in Shanghai.** I did not look pale on my face anymore. I had normal, healthy skin, like most young people my age. I need to thank XQ Chen and Guangning water pump factory for their hospitality during those months, which got me back to normal good health. XQ Chen was the manager of that factory at that time.

Life during those several months was lovely and peaceful, with good food. But I was also lonely in this small and remote town. Most of the time, I was the only guest in this factory's hostel, which had a dozen guest rooms. During weekends, I would watch some movies in nearby theaters or walk around this town's only main commercial street to better understand the local community. I could gradually understand the local dialect by watching local TV programs and listening to conversations among locals. Sometimes, I got bored and would walk into nearby villages. I climbed up nearby small hills by myself. I would sit at the top of the hill for a while, looking over the nearby towns and villages and wondering why I was here and what the future of my life and career would be. By the end of this business trip, the factory arranged a 2-day vacation visit for me to Zhaoqing (肇庆) as a reward. That was the first and only time I visited this thousands-old city, including the site of Qixingyan (七星岩).

10.3 Trip to Haikou and Sanya in Hainan Province

MA and Guangning Water Pump Factory were trying to build fast-speed boats for the border patrol troops in Hainan Province. At the beginning of June 1989, I got the chance to travel to Haiko and Sanya with colleagues, including teacher Zheng, LD Wen, and XQ Chen. That was the first and the only time I visited this tropical island. We rode a van from Guangning, stopped in Yanjiang City for lunch, and arrived at Zhangjiang port. We waited several hours in that port before boarding a boat to sail to Haiko, as too many vehicles were in line that day. Many people rushed to Hainan that year as it had just opened as a special economic zone in China. Haikou was much hotter than I expected in June. When we had meals with border troop soldiers, they would pour cold well water into porridge and cool it down before eating it, which tasted much better in the hot summer over there. During this trip, I met some business people whose parents were high-ranking government and military officials in China. It was common then in southern China for those people to succeed in business as they had much more privilege and connections than others. We got a chance to have a well-known Wenchang chicken in Haikou. After several days of stay in that city, we visited Sanya with the company of a border troop official. We stopped in a restaurant for lunch on the midway. The restaurant was located on a farm managed by people forced back from Indonesia in the 1960s. It was the first time I tasted curry chicken in that restaurant. I was also excited to see Wanquan River (万泉河), which was related to the popular ballet movie Red Detachment of Women (红色娘子军) and Nan Batian (南霸天) Sanya was beautiful with few tourists and nice beaches at that time, like Yalongwan (亚龙湾) and Tianyahaijiao (天涯海角) **While in Tianyahaijiao, I quietly sat on the beach, facing the open south ocean, and asked myself what the new world would look like behind those open oceans. It would be nice to have a chance to see those outside worlds if possible.** In the port of Sanya, controlled by the border troops, we saw some Vietnamese refugees who escaped from Vietnam on small boats. I got to talk briefly in English with a young Vietnamese girl who was around ten years old. They risked their lives to ride such a small boat across the South China Ocean to leave their country. They wanted to go to Hong Kong and then to Western countries like the USA or France. **I wondered why they wanted to take such a big risk, leaving behind everything they had in their hometown and going for a new life in a strange world.** Several years later, I met an EM colleague in Kansas City who was also a refugee from Vietnam and had a similar experience to this young girl. This colleague was lucky enough that his whole family moved to the USA with the help of US troops in 1976 when Xigong (西贡) fell.

Sanya Beach 1989 (LD Wen, S. Zheng, Walter)

10.4 Trip to Wenzhou in Zhejiang Province

In late 1989, I went on a business trip to Wenzhou with a colleague from MA. The customers were interested in building ships using water-jet propulsion technology suitable for shallow rivers like Oujiang. We arrived in Wenzhou and then traveled to a smaller river port inland by Oujiang. At that time, Wenzhou was well known for its family-owned small factories making shoes and clothes with primitive technology and equipment. Its economy stayed that way without many upgrades.

10.5 Colleagues and Friends In MA

Colleagues I got a chance to work with many good colleagues. LD Wen, my deputy advisor of graduate studies in MA, helped me greatly with my MS thesis research and engineering work in MA. He was sharp on people relations and marketing MA's technology and products. I very much appreciated his support throughout all those years. YB Su, YB Wan, and DJ Qian helped me obtain my passport faster when I tried to come to the USA for a Ph.D. study. YB Su was the director of MA then. XJ Shen, the head of the research and development department under MA, introduced me to Professor Bernard from the University of Iowa while he was visiting MA.

Friends FY Xie, my Tsinghua roommate and classmate, came to Shanghai in 1986 to enhance his English at Shanghai Foreign Language University for about one year. He was preparing for his graduate study in England, sponsored by the Petroleum Department of China. Therefore, BG Meng, MC Zhang, FY Xie, and I got chances to get together regularly, mainly in MA. All of us were in the same class in Tsinghua. BG was working full-time and had a better income than us. **He helped cover most of our food expenses at parties most of the time, and I appreciated it.** CB Xiao and I quickly became good friends while in our graduate studies. He continued pursuing his Ph.D. in SJTU after 1988 and got his degree in 1991 in thermal engineering. He was talented and should continue academic research at SJTU. Instead, he chose to go back to Zhangzhou City to have an opportunity to go abroad to continue his academic work, which turned into tragedy when he lost his life in 1993. I felt very sad to lose such a good friend. In 1999, I visited his mother in the Shili village of Changtai with QC Lin and TN, who were also graduates of SJTU. GA Ye was my high school classmate from Changtai. He graduated in 1985 and got a job in Shanghai's biggest retail store. His office was close to mine in Waitan. We got chances to see each other regularly. He cooked good meals when I visited him. We also went home together one year in 1989 during the Chinese New Year festival. DZ Li was studying for his MS degree in a research institute under the Chinese Academy of Science in Shanghai while I was doing mine during the period. We met while we attended the same class at SJTU. I learned that both of us were from the Mingnan area of Fujian. His family was in Xiamen City. In Shanghai, I also got to know a senior from Lindun called SC Lin. He graduated from college in the 1960s and worked at another research institute in Shanghai. His whole family was friendly to me, and I visited them regularly.

10.6 Difficult Decision to Stay or Leave Shanghai

After the trip from Guangdong and Hainan in June 1989, I had been struggling with what to do next. Should I continue a peaceful engineering life in MA or explore a new life outside Shanghai? Would it be better to go abroad to continue my academic study? At that time, the wave of going abroad was hot and popular. Almost everyone, especially young and educated people, was trying to leave China for a better future education. Those who succeeded in studying in Western and more developed countries were greatly envied by society. My mother and brothers also started to check if I had a girlfriend and the future marriage plan. One day during the break of Chinese New Year in 1990 in Lindun, I went alone to visit my father's graveyard in a nearby mountain valley. **I lay down by his grave for a long time, wondering what to do next, hoping to get some hints from my father. I fell asleep in the graveyard for a while and was awakened by birds chirping in nearby trees.** The weather was good that day, with a clear sky near noon.

During that period, SanGe ran into an older cousin of Amelia, who also lived in Lindun. They knew Amelia, and I attended the same elementary school from 1975 to 1976. The cousin told SanGe that Amelia still had not married and was studying for an MS degree at Fujian Normal University, majoring in English. She got her English BS degree from Fujian Normal University in 1986 and taught English at Zhangzhou Normal College for several years. This is a 4-year college now called Mingnan University. That college sponsored her to go back to Fujian Normal University to get her MS degree with an obligation to return to teach over there. Most girls in Changtai got married pretty young. Amelia's younger sister already had a stable boyfriend and was ready to get married. Later, ErGe wrote me a letter saying that he was asked if Amelia and I had an opportunity to develop our relationship further if I was not married. I knew this was the time I needed to make a critical decision. I realized this was the right moment to move on to a new chapter. After 1985, I started asking myself if I still had a home for myself. I did have an aged mother and dear brothers I would always like to be with. However, all brothers were separated, with each other having their own families. Mother was in Lindun all the time, mainly with SanGe, losing most of her working capacity at that age. **I had been drifting myself too long from age 13 and longed for a small nest to rest in when I was tired or sick.** A girl like Amelia was as nice and supportive as the most traditional ones from the south Fujian area. That was what I needed, as I had developed a strong character through many years of hardship, struggle, and exploration. This was meant to be. We had never spoken to each other before 1990, including in elementary school, like other boys and girls at that time, even though we had known each other from childhood. Life brought us together many years later. We started communicating by letters first and then by phone occasionally as it was expensive. The communication was easy as we came from the same hometown and had similar backgrounds. Both of us were old and mature enough to know what we needed then.

Visit to Fuzhou I visited Amelia in Fuzhou in May 1990. Fuzhou was the capital city of Fujian Province, where Amelia studied for her MS degree at Fujian Normal University. That was the first time I visited that city and Fujian Normal University. Overall, I had a good impression of this city. It was clean and green with many trees and delicious foods. I got a chance to meet my high school classmates, MS Shen and LS Ye. LS had just become a father. MS married a sweet girl and was preparing to be a father.

Visit to Zhangzhou City, Dongshan, and Zhangpu Counties

During the Chinese New Year's break of 1991. Amelia and I got the marriage certificate in Zhangzhou City. That was the first time I wore a suit and a tie, which was needed for the marriage certificate photo. By then, Amelia had graduated from Fujian Normal University with an MS degree and was teaching in the English department of Zhangzhou Normal College. **That was the first time I visited Zhangzhou City.** Zhangzhou City was a small and peaceful city at that time. I liked the beef noodle soup over there. I also saw QC Lin, SY Dai, and WH Huang. SY and WH were my high school classmates. Amelia and I visited Dongshan County during that period, which was several hours away from Zhangzhou

City by public bus. Amelia later needed to bring her students to a training class in a high school in Zhangpu County, located by the ocean. I went with her for several days as I was still on vacation.

Family in Lindun's House (1991, Mother and Brothers)

The above photo was taken at the top of the house. It showed downtown buildings on the only commercial street.

Amelia also visited me in Shanghai during the summer of 1991. Her parents joined later. We went to visit Hangzhou before Amelia's parents headed back to Changtai.

Chapter 11
Challenging Journey to the USA

After Amelia and I started dating long distance between Shanghai and Fuzhou, we realized the road to our union was tough. There were few career opportunities for me in Zhangzhou, and I would probably not be able to get used to life in such a small place after living in Beijing and Shanghai for so many years. At the same time, it was extremely difficult for Amelia to move to Shanghai as there was strict residency control in Shanghai. Some colleagues in MA had separated from their wives and kids in different cities for many years because they could not move to Shanghai. This left us the only better option of going abroad to study together, as many young and educated people did at that time. It was a very risky decision at that time. Our life would be much harder if we failed to come to the USA. MW Zhang, my roommate in MA, went to the Netherlands as an exchange scholar in 1989. MJ Yang, in Xiamen, had an opportunity to study for a Ph.D. at the University of Chicago in 1990. YQ Qin, who is from MA, and DZ Li, who is from Xiamen, also studied in the USA around 1991. Their success gave me much encouragement. CB Xiao and many graduate students at SJTU were also preparing to study abroad.

11.1 Graduate Application

I started intensive preparation for the TOEFL and GREs at Qiangjing Language School in Shanghai sometime in 1990. The class was in the evening after work. I met SJ Liang from that class. By then, I had lived a relatively relaxed life since 1986 without attending a class and preparing for exams. I felt uneasy at the beginning of going back to the classroom. **My heart rate started to go up sharply sometime that year and was mostly at 90 to 100 for more**

than 30 years up to 2021 before I resigned from my job. It was at 100 during my physical exam in January 1992. After the TOEFL and GREs, I started applying to universities in the USA. The application fees were between US$25.00 and US$40.00 at that time, which was very expensive to me as my monthly salary was less than US$15.00 at that time. TOEFL and GRE fees were also expensive at US$30.00 to US$50.00. I applied to about ten universities, which pretty much used up all my savings. It was also difficult to get US dollars in Shanghai. I had to get some of them from a businessman with a ratio of 1 to 8 (one US dollar for 8 RMB). **I appreciated that YQ Qin and DZ Li helped me pay some application fees as both were already in the USA then. CY Shen helped me obtain and pay for official transcripts from Tsinghua, which were needed for the applications.**

11.2 Painful Process to Get a Passport

By the spring of 1991, I got admitted to several universities in the USA without any financial assistance, including the Department of Mechanical Engineering at The University of Iowa. The school started in the Fall of 1991, meaning I needed to apply for a passport and find any financial sponsorship as soon as possible. It was difficult for a mechanical engineering graduate to receive a scholarship or financial assistantship from universities and professors then. In the early 1990s, it was extremely difficult to get a passport in China as I had an MS degree and a middle-level engineer title (中级工程师职称). I had to delay the start of school until spring 1992 because of the availability of a passport. **The following were the steps I went through to get a passport:**

i. Showed that I had an overseas relative as I had not worked up to five years after graduating with my MS degree in May 1988. Amelia's father helped obtain it. I was prepared to continue the effort to study abroad after five years of service if this document could not be obtained.

ii. Obtained written official permission from MA's personnel department: The director of MA was very helpful, probably because he was also from the south Fujian area. Other colleagues in MA helped, too, based on friendship and kindness.

iii. Paid back a portion of my education fees as I had not served up to a five-year term, which accounted for several years' annual income for me at that time. **I had to borrow a lot of money from a family friend in Changtai, which took me a while to pay back after arriving in the USA. A one-way air ticket from Shanghai to Chicago alone cost around US$1000.00 in 1992. My monthly salary in MA was only US$15.00 in 1991.**

iv. Obtained written official permission from CSS, which managed MA. CSS was a cabinet-level ministry in central government at that time. In November 1991, I stayed in Beijing anxiously for more than one week to wait for written permission with the help of TC Han and WZ Zai. Both had worked in MA for a short period of rotation training right after joining CSS. The weather in Beijing was cold, and the sky was grey and full of dust, probably because of heating from coal. I saw CY and BZ Zhu one evening during that week in CY's apartment home on the Tsinghua campus. BZ was also my classmate in Tsinghua. CY was doing his postdoctoral research, and BZ was doing his Ph.D. study at Tsinghua.

v. Obtained written official permission from the Higher Education Department of Shanghai: DJ Qian from MA introduced her friend to me in that department, which facilitated the process. I received a full financial assistantship from the University of Iowa in September 1991. The staff member in the department who handled my application said it was rare for him to see that an engineering graduate student could obtain a full financial assistantship from a USA university at that time.

vi. Applied for a passport from the Shanghai Public Safety Department: YB Wan from MA helped facilitate it as he had a relative working in that department.

11.3 Difficulty in Finding Financial Sponsorship and Assistantship

At that time, anyone admitted to US universities without financial sponsorship and assistantship could not receive a visa from the US embassy. LC Wen, a friend of FZ Wang in Hong Kong, provided me with a strong financial affidavit. Teacher Zheng was working with FZ Wang on some projects. They were friends back in MA many years ago. LC Wen was the chief engineer in XG Group under the Gambling King in Macao. He spent several hours in the US general consulate in Hong Kong to obtain the affidavit I intended to use to apply for my visa. LC Wen later gave me US$500.00 in financial support, like a personal scholarship, through FZ Wang right before I left Shanghai for the USA. In parallel to the effort by LC Wen, Amelia's father also helped obtain another financial affidavit from our hometown senior, CX Liang. CX Liang was the police chief of Changtai District before 1949 and escaped to Taiwan afterward. Eventually, I did not use both affidavits as I received a full financial assistantship from the University of Iowa, as below. I sincerely appreciate their efforts. **After I got my first job in the USA, I donated several times to "Hope Elementary Schools" in rural China by mailing checks directly to them around 2000. I could not stand poor students quitting school because of a bad family economy. Before I resigned from LE VE in October 2021, I also continuously**

donated for over 15 years to many programs and persons who badly needed financial support. They included the charity organizations of United Way in Ohio, families in the USA like Sherry Chen, a food pantry program in Columbus, Ohio, the National Chinese Association (NCA) in the USA, the 80-20 Initiative, and a Chinese School in Columbus, Ohio.

In the summer of 1991, two professors from the University of Iowa, Dr. VP and Dr. Bernard, visited MA for academic exchange. They were invited by XJ Shen, who was the head of a research department in MA. I was admitted to the University of Iowa then and could not get a visa without financial support. As a private tutor in high school back in the 1950s for XJ Shen, Teacher Zheng had a special relationship with him. I talked to XJ Shen directly about my situation, and he happily introduced me to both professors. I accompanied both professors to watch an acrobatics show (杂技) in Shanghai and explained my application situation to them. I also showed them my research and work experience. At that time, Professor Bernard was looking for Ph.D. students in CFD (Computational Fluid Dynamics). He agreed to look at my application after they were back in the USA. My BS thesis research in Tsinghua probably impressed him as it involved a similar simulation method of fluid mechanics and hydrodynamics in FEA (Finite Element Analysis). In September 1991, I received a full assistantship from The University of Iowa and Professor Bernard, which was extremely important to Amelia and me. It included 50% Research Assistantship (RA) and 50% Teaching Assistantship (TA). I could also postpone my studies until spring 1992, as I still needed my passport and visa. I should mention that Professor C. Shen, my future Ph.D. advisor in the USA, was the chairman of the Department of Mechanical Engineering at the University of Iowa at that time. He supported my admission and assistantship from that department and Professor Bernard as the department chairman. **Somehow, with luck, I ran into Professor**

Shen, who eventually became another critical person in my life (贵人) after Teacher Zheng.

11.4 Trip Back to Changtai and Wedding

After receiving the passport and financial assistantship, I felt more confident I could study in the USA. I returned to Changtai in January 1992 to say goodbye to families and had an official wedding with Amelia. The wedding was much bigger than I expected and caused some misunderstandings among relatives, which I regretted. It was quite emotional to say goodbye to families, especially my mother. I did not expect that I would not be able to see them again until December 1999, almost eight years later. Amelia traveled with me back to Shanghai after the wedding. It should be mentioned that CW Zhao from Changtai, a well-known entrepreneur in Changtai, kindly provided US$300.00 during the wedding to assist with my trip to the USA, which I appreciated.

Wedding in Yanxi with Family (January 1992)

11.5 A Visa to The USA

On Jan 17, 1992, I went to the US general consulate in Shanghai to apply for a visa from the USA. It was an early and sunny morning. There was a long line at the front gate of the consulate. People in the line were very nervous. They were worried they would be rejected, as had happened to most applicants. The approval rate was very low at that time, like a lottery. I could see most people in front of me came out disappointed. Some in the line asked them why they were rejected. The most common answer was, "You have an immigration intention." I went in to meet a young male American and handed over all of my documents. After reviewing them, he asked me two simple questions in English: Did you graduate from Tsinghua? Will you go for a Ph.D. study at the University of Iowa? After receiving the yes answer, he took a note, stamped my visa, and said, "Welcome to the USA." I said, "Thank you," and happily came out. People still waiting in that long line outside the consulate saw my smiling face and understood I had got my visa. Some asked me, and I told them I would pursue a Ph.D. study with a full financial assistantship. They nodded and said that was why you got the visa.

11.6 Departure of China to The University of Iowa in January 1992

After receiving the visa, I quickly contacted SJ Liang, whom I knew from Qianjing school, to book the air ticket to the USA. She was working in China Eastern Airlines at that time. It was difficult to find an international air ticket without any connection then, probably with limited airliners for international flights. I also borrowed enough money to purchase a lot of daily necessities such as clothes, shoes, toothpaste, medicines, and others, as I was told that everything would be much more expensive in the USA. It was the first time I shopped for myself as I did not know how to buy appropriate items before as a bachelor. SiGe traveled from Wuyan County to see me off as we had not seen each other for a while. In late January 1992, I departed Shanghai for the University of Iowa through San Francisco and Chicago. I had been late for the spring semester for several weeks and had a lot to catch up on.

Part II – Life in the USA

Chapter 12
Ph.D. Study from 1992 to 1997

12.1 Travel to the University of Iowa by Airplane and Greyhound in January 1992

In late January of 1992, I left Shanghai Hongqiao Airport at about noon time for San Francisco. This was the first time I boarded an airplane and the first time I left China. Amelia, SiGe, several MA colleagues, and friends saw me off at the airport. When the aircraft left the airport and headed for the ocean direction, I looked over the window and wondered when I could be back. It was quite emotional, excited, and nervous as too many unknowns were ahead. It took almost 15 hours to fly from Shanghai to San Francisco. I arrived in San Francisco early on the 2nd day, filled out forms, got stamped on entry to the USA, and passed through customs. I needed to wait several hours at the airport before boarding another airplane to Chicago. Part of San Francisco could be seen from the airport terminal, and it felt cold. It was winter, and there was not much green. I had contacted MJ Yang ahead of time from Shanghai and at San Francisco airport about my arrival. MJ and his wife, ZY Yang, came to pick me up from the airport late at night. After staying at MJ's place for two nights, I took a Greyhound to the University of Iowa in Iowa City, about four hours away from Chicago. There was no airport in Iowa City as it was too small, with only about fifty thousand people during the academic year. The bus passed through mostly rural and remote areas in Illinois and Iowa and frequently stopped at small towns to drop off and pick up passengers. I was the only Asian on the bus, which was full of people of different colors and skins. Some young people had small pieces of red hair on the top of their shaved heads. The first impression was most people had rosy faces, probably because they ate more meat and protein than people in China. **I felt a bit nervous and** lonely on the 3rd day outside China and on this unfamiliar remote land, a similar feeling to what I had in the summer of 1980 when I traveled alone from Lindun to attend Tsinghua University in Beijing. I did fall asleep most of the time on the bus due to jet lag. From MJ's place, I called the contact person in the Chinese Student's Association at the University of Iowa ahead of time. HQ greeted me at the Greyhound station because he was the leader of that group. He helped me find an apartment in Ellis Place and sent me over that evening.

12.2 Life in Iowa City from 1992 to 1993

12.2.1 Short of Money to Pay Three Month Rent on First Day

Ellis Place was an apartment building full of singles. Many of them were Chinese students like me. I lived in a room of about 12 square meters on the 3rd floor with a refrigerator from the landlord. There was a public bathroom on each floor. All tenants had a shared kitchen in the basement. The rent was about US$150.00 per month for this unfurnished room. The previous tenant was also a Chinese student who left me with an old twin mattress so I could sleep on the floor. He also gave me an old chair and a simple table to eat and study. The building, including my room, was full of big roaches (蟑螂), probably because there was a lot of wasted food inside the building. I could see and feel them at night when I slept, even on my mattress. A Chinese student took me to shop for food and other daily necessities that night. He told me I could ask others to help me once by telling them I was a new student coming to the USA. He also took me to sign a rental lease at the owner's home. **It caught me by surprise that I was asked to pay three months' rent at once: one for the last month of the 12-month lease, one for the security deposit, and one for the first month. I did not have enough money to pay for all three months and asked for a delayed**

payment from the landlord. That was a difficult night for me as I had nowhere to find the money as a newcomer to the USA. **I could not sleep well that night as I did not know how to handle this situation.** Someone told me later that the International Student Office at the university might be able to help. As there was no other option, I went to seek help on the 2nd day. Fortunately, I did get a US$500.00 loan because they knew I could pay back through my RA (Research Assistantship) and TA (Teaching Assistantship) salary income soon. This was the first culture shock for me financially because I did not know I had to pay three months' rent at once or else I would have borrowed more money in Changtai. As a new foreign student, borrowing money from others in this credit-based society was hard. **From that moment, I was very careful with future budget plans and always conservative and frugal to account for any possible unknowns that might put me and my family in a similar difficult position.**

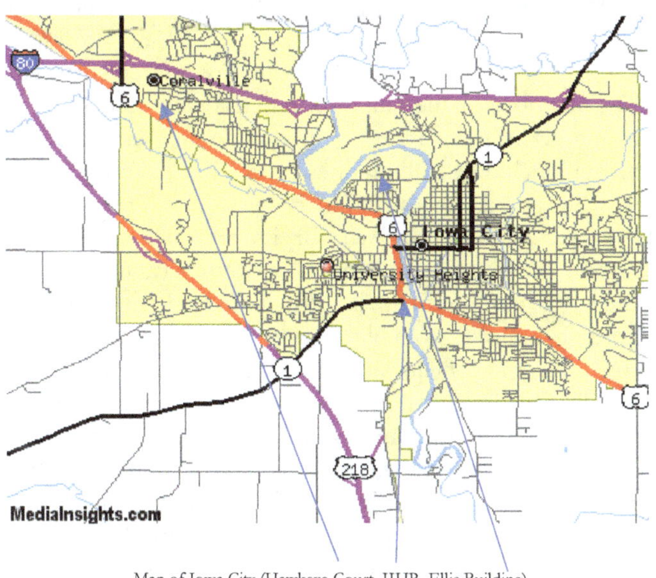

Map of Iowa City (Hawkeye Court, IIHR, Ellis Building)

On the 2nd day, I walked to IIHR (Iowa Institute of

Hydraulic Research) to see Professor Bernard. He was happy to see me at the University of Iowa. I was several weeks late for school and needed to report to the international student office for permission to start my studies. The office asked me to take the Foreign Languages Test immediately, which was required for anyone like me just coming to the USA. I passed in a sleepy mood due to jet lag and was able to register for classes for that semester. This meant that I could also start working on my research and teaching assistantship jobs with a legal working status (F-1) to get paid soon. The first several weeks were very stressful as I needed to catch up on each class and prepare to learn a new job as a research and teaching assistant. I did not know how I survived those months, and I was relieved to reach the end of that semester in May 1992.

12.2.2 The University of Iowa and Iowa City

IIHR was a world-leading institute on hydraulics and hydrodynamics at that time. Its director, Professor Kennedy, was the World's Hydraulic Committee chairman and a member of the Engineering Academy of USA. For many years, this institute has attracted many international scholars, including leading ones from China, like Professor Qian Ning and Professor Lin Binnan. The University of Iowa was also well-known for its creative writing and Astronomy physics programs. Unfortunately, in 1991, A Chinese Ph.D. student in Physics killed five people, including himself, possibly because of mental illness like depression and loneliness. He had almost no friends and isolated himself for a long time. Three of the victims were the world's leading scholars in astronomy and physics, including his Ph.D. advisor and a vice president of the University of Iowa. One fellow Chinese Ph.D. graduate was also the victim. I learned this bad news from Shanghai by the end of 1991 before I planned to leave for the University of Iowa for my Ph.D. study. This event placed a sad shadow and had a chilling effect on the Chinese students at the

University of Iowa. Iowa City itself was a small college town with a population of about 50,000. Among them, 30,000 were students. It was very cold in winter with much snow. There was no Chinese store as only several hundred Chinese people lived in this town.

12.2.3 Curriculum in The Department of Mechanical Engineering

I was admitted into the Fluid and Thermal Science major of the Mechanical Engineering Department at the University of Iowa. I was good at fluid mechanics as I had been in hydraulic and ocean engineering at Tsinghua and SJTU. However, thermal science was new to me. I had to pick it up soon in my Ph.D. study, including thermodynamics and heat transfer. Heat transfer includes radiation, convection, and conduction. It was a shock to me that the textbooks were so expensive. I spent more than US$300.00 to buy three textbooks on thermodynamics, heat transfer, and aerodynamics classes in the first semester. The monthly rent was about US$150.00. My English was considered good in China. However, that was not good enough for almost all international students in the first several years in the USA. I did not fully understand what professors said in the classrooms and needed to study the textbooks in detail after the classes. Because they were also in new technical fields, sometimes I spent more than one hour reading and understanding the key content on one page. Most of the time, I would walk alone for more than 35 minutes at night along the road covered with heavy snow to study in the cubic office of the IIHR building. I did not have a car until the summer of 1992.

12.2.4 Learning to Cook

I had not had a chance to learn how to cook real food before I came to the USA in 1992. I only helped cook porridge and fried vegetables in Lindun before 1978, as my mother or my older brothers would cook better foods for holidays or guest parties. In Tsinghua, I did not even know noodles should not be put into cold water initially. In the basement kitchen of that Ellis apartment building in Iowa, there were multiple stoves for several people to cook simultaneously, mostly in the evening. I would observe them and learn by trial and error based on different combinations of meat, vegetables, and seasoning, like salt, spices, and soy sources. Fortunately, milk, egg, and chicken were cheap. I got to eat a lot of them, which was very good for my health. I tried to eat like an American, drinking cold milk directly from the refrigerator and eating bananas along with it in the morning, which might have damaged my stomach without my knowledge at that time. I also learned how to cook rice from a microwave, which was easy and quick. Like most students, I prepared enough food for three to four days at a time and cooked only about two times per week. After 6 to 12 months, I became a good cook among Chinese students as I treated cooking as a chemical experiment to try different recipes and combinations of different ingredients.

12.2.5 My First Car

In the summer of 1992, I saved enough money to buy a cheap car as Amelia would join me in Iowa. Before that, I needed to go shopping weekly in a car with the help of others. **My first car was an old Mercury from a graduate student who was going to leave the USA. It cost me US$1200.00.** I was excited to own a car and took a picture to show to my family in China. A friend, KJ Gao, showed me how to start the car and accompanied me several times to drive around in parking lots. Then, I started practicing myself without going to any driving school as it was too expensive for most international students.

12.2.6 Joining of Amelia and New Apartment

Soon after I arrived at the University of Iowa, I sent out the official invitation letter to Amelia with official documents from the University of Iowa so she could apply for her passport and visa to the USA. In the summer of 1992, she arrived at Cedar Rapids airport, about 45 miles from Iowa City. I proudly drove that Mercury to pick her up. I also picked up another Chinese student, JX Dong, who would study chemistry at the University of Iowa. Amelia and JX met during the trip. JX happened to be from Yongan Fujian. Amelia also brought a three-year-old girl, the daughter of another Chinese graduate student, to the University of Iowa. Her parents were from Xiamen, Fujian. They left their daughter behind in China at that time. I got to know them during the spring semester of 1992. When they learned that Amelia would join me in Iowa, they asked Amelia to help them bring their daughter back to them, which could save them a big trip.

As a married couple, we were qualified to move into a family apartment in Hawkeye Court, located in another small town of Coralville near Iowa City. Hawkeye Court was about 10 miles away from the IIHR building. There were hundreds of apartments surrounded by farm fields in Hawkeye Court. Those were university-owned apartments for married students. We stayed in a one-bedroom apartment of about 70 square meters on the 2nd floor of an apartment building. There was one bedroom, a restroom, and a living room with a kitchen. The apartment was clean. It had central heating and 24-hour hot water for baths and washing. A refrigerator, electric stove, a baking oven, and a phone were also provided. It was unfurnished without an air-conditioner. The rent was about US$210.00 per month, which was probably a discounted price for married students from the university. We bought some old and simple furniture from a yard sale, including a mattress, one old sofa, one simple table for meals, and several small chairs. SF Xu, a Ph.D. student in IIHR from Taiwan, nicely provided us with some old window curtains. It was a dream apartment, and we were pretty happy. I could not imagine having such a nice, spacious apartment in Shanghai then.

12.2.7 Car Breakdown Accident and Disappearance of Car on Highway at Night

One evening in the winter of 1992, I drove to the IIHR building to study and work after dinner. My car suddenly broke down on a remote uphill road between Iowa City and Coralville. I walked around looking for help in nearby apartments so I could call my friends, which took me around 20 minutes. **When I finally made a call and returned to the road, my car disappeared. I panicked and did not understand how my car had been gone in such a short period of time.** One friend came from IIHR to pick me up and sent me home shortly. I had a long night that day. I talked to several friends and was told that the best chance was to call the city police on the 2nd day. Fortunately, I found out later that the city had towed my car because they did not allow a broken vehicle to block the road. With the help of a friend who gave me a ride to that tow company, I paid the towing fee and was able to tow my broken car with AAA (American Automobile Association) to a nearby mechanic. It was found that there was an issue with the transmission, which cost me several hundred dollars to fix. I got my car back on the 3rd day and drove it for only two days before it broke down again. I was quite upset that the mechanics did not fix the problem. I asked an American classmate to accompany me to see the mechanics in case they took advantage of a foreign student. After two more days, I got my car back again. It worked fine after that.

12.2.8 Ph.D. Qualifying exam

I was allowed to postpone my Ph.D. qualifying exam to fall 1992 with the permission of the department chairman,

Professor C. Shen. This exam was the most important and difficult part of a Ph.D. study at any major US university. I worked hard on thermal science courses and did very well on this exam, which covered math, fluid mechanics, thermos science, and others. I was told I might achieve one of the highest scores in department history, which later led to a potential misunderstanding among my research team.

Ellis Apartment (Feb 1992)

IIHR Building (March 1992)

First Car Summer 1992 (Hawkeye Apartment)

Front of Hawkeye Apt.

Campus of Iowa (summer 1992)

12.2.9 Research Assistant and Ph.D. Research Direction

I was very lucky to receive an RA (Research Assistantship) and a TA (Teaching Assistantship) in Shanghai to get a visa to the USA. In return, I was required to work 10 hours on RA and 10 hours on TA each semester, in addition to taking all the courses. The research direction was on CFD (Computational Fluid Dynamics), which was very hot in the 1990s, especially in fluid dynamics and hydraulics. Professor Bernard got a big grant and a project from the Navy lab, which required much work. CFD was new, and I had to learn from the beginning. I could only do some supporting work for the first semester as I had not taken CFD courses yet. Before contributing, I had to understand the theoretical physics, methodology, and detailed coding.

12.2.10 Teaching Assistant

My first TA course was Thermodynamics for undergraduates. VP Basu, another graduate student, and I helped Professor Bernard in this class, grading homework and providing official hours to students with questions. VP would be my future Ph.D. classmate with Dean Shen at FSU. There were more than one hundred students in this class. Thermodynamics was new to me, too. I bought a textbook and studied it intensively under great pressure for my TA work.

12.2.11 Friends

One day in the spring semester of 1992, KJ Gao suddenly came to me to ask if he could stay with me for a few days in that 12-square-meter room before he found a place to live. He had lived in a 3-bedroom basement apartment with two Chinese students. One roommate's husband had joined his wife just a few weeks ago from

Shenzhen and hanged himself in the storage room of that basement. KJ could not stay in that room anymore as he sometimes heard a crying sound from that storage room since the accident.

We got to know SJ Zeng and his family as he was from a town in Anxi County, which was only about 20 kilometers away from Lindun. SJ and his wife graduated from Fujian Normal University in China. His wife was also in the same English Department as Amelia. We met again in Kansas City in 1997 when I got my first industry job in the USA.

In the summer of 1993, several old friends from Tsinghua and Zhangzhou gathered in Milwaukee, including Amelia and the wives of PW Liu and FS Zhuang. PH Huang and TH Huang were studying at the University of Milwaukee then. We all stayed overnight in their two-bedroom apartment.

Soon after I came to the University of Iowa, DZ Li, a friend back in Shanghai, visited me in Iowa City with his wife, FZ. They were studying for their Ph.D. at the University of Wisconsin.DZ introduced me to one of their friends who was also studying at the University of Iowa. **They took me to a buffet lunch, which was my first buffet and restaurant experience in the USA.**

12.2.12 Amelia's Adjustment to New Life in the USA

With an F2 visa, Amelia was not allowed to work in any jobs in the USA. We were also too poor to pay out-of-state tuition for her to attend any classes. Amelia mostly stayed home while I was busy with my RA, TA, and heavy schoolwork. This was a difficult period for wives who had just come to the USA with their husbands to study at a university. She envied many of those who had jobs, even those who worked as a waitress in restaurants. She often hung out with a friend, discussing how they could find any job.

12.2.13 Difficult Decision to Transfer to FSU with Dean Shen

I passed my Ph.D. qualifying exam at the end of 1992 with probably one of the best scores in the department's history, which was even a bit of a surprise to me as thermal science was a new area. However, this also led to a misunderstanding among some research team members. They thought I spent too much time studying and not enough time on research. This might be due to cultural differences. I thought a strong foundation in basic science in my area was needed to prepare myself to do better research and contribute to the ongoing project. I started having an uneasy relationship with some team members and felt stressed and pressured. I was afraid I might lose my jobs as RA and TA, which would be a disaster because I could not pay tuition and living costs. **I could not work outside the university campus with an F1 student visa at that time. Amelia could not work at all with an F2 visa. The only possible income would be from a campus job in the university cafeteria, laundry, and university building as a janitor. I checked some of them and took home some application forms in case I needed them while continuing to work in the current research team.** During that period, Professor C. Shen, the department chairman of Mechanical Engineering at the University of Iowa, moved to FSU to be Dean of the Engineering College. I contacted him and asked if I could go with him to continue my Ph.D. study under him. Several weeks later, I was lucky to receive his yes reply. We had lunch in a Chinese restaurant called YuanJin with other future Ph.D. students before we moved to FSU. These future Ph.D. classmates were KC Anderson from Iowa, YH Saleh from Jordan, and VP Basu from India. That was the 2nd time and only time I ate in a Chinese restaurant in Iowa City.

I looked back at what happened with the research team many years later. It would have been better to communicate more effectively with my team and fully explain my plan to do better research. My English communication skills and understanding of American culture in university research were limited then. After I worked as a professor at SJTU from 2003 to 2004, I better understood the pressure a professor had, including seeking funding and delivering on projects. After I finished my Ph.D. with Dean Shen and started my postdoctoral research at UIUC, I emailed Professor Bernard and other previous research team members to inform my status and thank them for their help during my stay with them at the University of Iowa and IIHR. **I deeply appreciated Professor Bernard's offer of RA and TA jobs in 1991 while I was still in Shanghai. Otherwise, my path to the USA for my Ph.D. study would have been much harder.**

12.3 Life in Tallahassee from 1993 to 1997

12.3.1 Travel to Florida State University by an Overnight Greyhound

In the summer of 1993, Amelia and I needed to move from the University of Iowa in Iowa City to Florida State University (FSU) in Tallahassee, Florida. Our car was too old to drive such a long distance, and I had no long-distance driving experience. So, we sold our car and traveled by Greyhound. We mailed most of the heavy items by the post office to the Department of Mechanical Engineering office in FSU and carried only valuable items with us on the road. We left Iowa City at noon and arrived at Chicago Greyhound station in the evening, the same one I used to leave Chicago for Iowa City in January 1992. Then, we boarded a greyhound in the late evening from Chicago and arrived in Tallahassee (Florida) at noon on the 2nd day. The bus stopped by several major cities, such as St. Louis, Nashville, Birmingham, and Montgomery, to drop off and pick up passengers. It passed some mountainous and flattened areas in total darkness. Most passengers, including us, slept on the bus. I woke up several times and watched over the nearby mountains and small towns through the window. **Similar to what I had in January 1992 when traveling from Chicago to Iowa City by myself on the bus, I felt nervous again during the trip when observing that we were the only Asians on the bus, traveling in total darkness in remote areas. Amelia was sleeping most of the time. At that moment, I felt Amelia and I were the only people in the world to rely on each other (相依为命). I wondered if it was worth it for us to give up all we had fought in China and come to the US to live such a life as a student.** However, life needed to move on, and there was no going back. Like many immigrants, we were exploring and continuing to seek a new and better life in this new land.

Finally, we arrived at the bus station in downtown Tallahassee, where FSU was located. I contacted the Chinese Student Association at FSU before the trip. Someone came to pick us up and sent us to a house several miles from campus. We could not go anywhere without a car that day. I applied for a family student apartment at FSU while we were still in Iowa. Fortunately, the FSU alumni village had an opening, so we moved into a two-bedroom apartment on the 2nd day. YZ helped us a lot during those days, including moving and shopping, as we did not have a car. He was a Ph.D. student in the department of mechanical engineering. We quickly shopped around and bought a Volkswagen car at US$1600.00. The air conditioner was broken, and we did not fix it as it would cost US$500.00, which was too expensive for a student like me then.

12.3.2 Tallahassee Florida

Tallahassee is the capital of Florida and had a population

of around 300,000 then. There were small Chinese grocery stores and more than 20 Chinese restaurants, which provided some working opportunities for some wives of Chinese graduate students. There were two major universities, FSU and FAMU (Florida Agricultural and Mechanical Universities). FAMU-FSU College of Engineering was jointly owned and operated by two universities. Dean Shen was an appointment from FSU. There were mechanical, civil, electric, industrial, and chemical engineering departments in this college. The college had about 100 faculty members, several hundred staff members, and more than two thousand students.

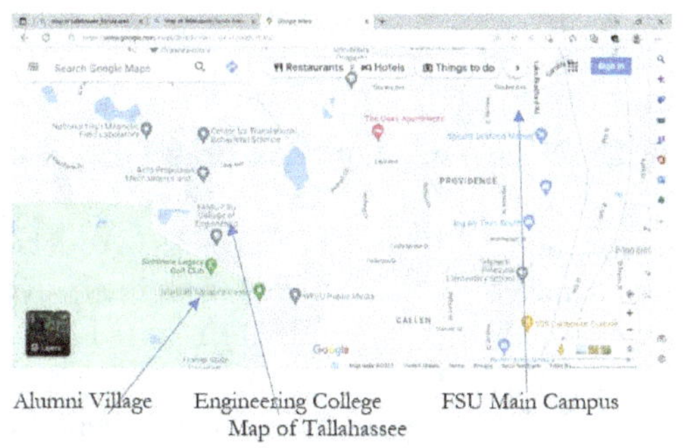

Alumni Village   Engineering College   FSU Main Campus
Map of Tallahassee

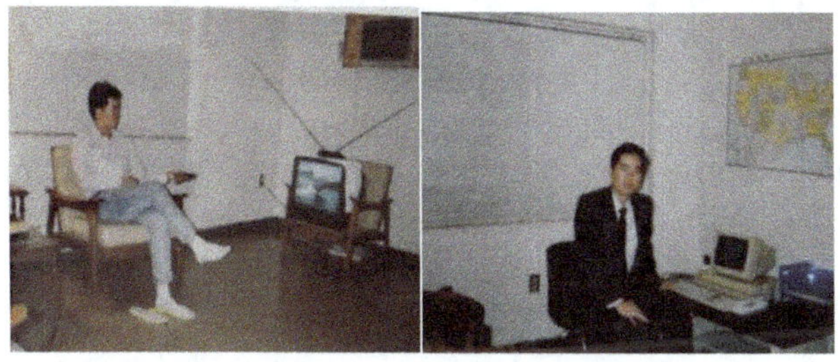

Apartment in Alumni Village Tallahassee 1993

Alumni Village was an apartment compound for FSU that housed graduate students and their families at a discounted rent. It sat nicely near FAMU - FSU College of Engineering. This compound had hundreds of apartments, becoming a major community for graduate and international students. Amelia and I moved into a two-bedroom apartment partially furnished with one full-size bed and mattress, one simple dining table, and several chairs. There was a refrigerator, a gas stove, and a baking oven. The laundry room was in another building inside Alumni Village. The rent for the first year was around US$270.00 per month. The building was built in the 1950s and had a central gas heating system during the winter season. This showed the big difference in living standards between the USA and China. There was still no central gas heating system in southern China during the winter up until 2020 in places like Shanghai, Nanjing, Wuhan, and Xiamen. Florida is more like Fujian and Guangdong in terms of climate.

12.3.3 Ph.D. Classmates and Research Direction

In the summer of 1993, YH Saleh, KC Anderson, and VP Basu transferred with Dean Shen from the University of Iowa to continue their Ph.D. study at FSU. As I had finished most courses at the University of Iowa and passed the Ph.D. qualifying exam, FSU waived my Ph.D. qualifying exam and accepted most of the courses I finished there. That helped me a lot in focusing on my research. Dean Shen was internationally well-known in thermal science and CFD in the 1990s, especially for the FA (Finite Analytic) method. I naturally chose to continue CFD and thermal science research for my Ph.D. with KC Anderson. YK and VP eventually picked biomedical science as their direction, which was good for them

12.3.4 Teaching Assistant Experience

Dean Shen did not have funded projects from any sponsors, so I needed to work as a TA to get a financial assistantship. Besides Thermodynamics and Heat Transfer for undergraduate classes, I was a TA on graduate math classes for several years. I was surprised to find that most graduates in engineering schools in the USA had mediocre math backgrounds.

12.3.5 ER Visit for Severe Duodenal Bleeding and Round Trip to Heaven

In Oct 1994, I felt sick for several days with a low fever and took some old medicines I had brought from China back in early 1992. The situation did not improve while I continued school and TA work. One afternoon, on the way to engineering school by the Alumni village, I felt dizzy and almost fell. I quickly called Amelia, who drove me to the emergency room at Tallahassee Memorial Hospital. I was admitted to the emergency room right away and went through a series of exams, including CT, blood work, et al. The doctor told me I was bleeding somewhere in my body, which reminded me that I had seen black stool over the past several days. I was hospitalized that night as I was very weak and could hardly stand up to those exams. **At midnight, while a nurse was helping me, I suddenly felt bad and said, "I do not feel good," and fell back to bed. The nurse shouted at others, yelling, "I need help here right away," Simultaneously, she told me, "Hold on to yourself. you are too young to go." I lost consciousness right after hearing those words from the nurse.** Probably after several hours, I became conscious again. Another nurse said, "You had a rough time last night." I did not know what medical staff in the best hospital in Tallahassee did to rescue me that night. In the morning, a group of doctors from different specialties visited me and discussed my situation as a group diagnosis. They told me that I had lost too much blood over the last few days and needed a blood transfusion right away. **That night was very dangerous to me. I almost lost my life due to huge blood loss. If I had not been in this hospital, I could have gone to heaven on that day.** I was arranged to have an endoscopy after many blood transfusions, and it was found that I had severe duodenal ulcer bleeding. During that day in that hospital, I heard some women in a nearby room crying and shouting, "You son of bitch, how can you leave me like that." The nurse told me that someone just passed away in the company of family members. **That day was quite emotional for me. I lay on the bed, watched up at the ceiling, and thought a lot about the life journey I had so far. My life could have been ended that night. Here, I thank those physicians, medical staff, and the hospital for saving my life, including the person who donated his or her blood to me. That person's blood is still flowing in my body.** Until now, I still do not quite understand how this severe duodenal ulcer bleeding occurred to me. The doctors told me at that time it could be the stress. I suspected that the old and expired medicines I took in those days may also be one of the factors. In addition, I started having spicy food in 1980 in Tsinghua, and I had cold milk and bananas after coming to the USA in 1992. All of them may have contributed to the damage to my stomach. I was too young to understand how to take care of my health before. I felt invincible before that time and learned a heavy lesson from this accident and sickness. Life is fragile and precious.

12.3.6 Birth of Daughter and ICU Stay

Dean Shen allowed me to slow down on research after the hospitalization in October 1994 so that I recovered well in several months, though my body still was quite weak. For the first time since 1990, I had some free time to rethink life. Amelia and I decided it was the right time to have a kid, as we were no longer young. By then, we had paid off my debt in China for my travel expenses to the USA and the education fee to MA because I did not have 5-year service yet. Amelia got pregnant in April 1995. That was a happy period we had as a future parent. We fully enjoyed peaceful and poor student life in Tallahassee. Our daughter, Sophia, was finally born at 4:34 pm, February 7, 1996, 2 weeks earlier than the due date. She weighed 6 lbs. and 11 ounces.

Sophia had difficulty breathing at birth. **She could not cry, and her whole body suddenly turned grey and bloodless right after birth**. Fortunately, the nurse was experienced. She grabbed both her legs quickly, hit her body gently, and said, "Come on." Moments later, Sophia cried, and her body turned back to a normal body color. **I was shocked, scared, and speechless in front of both my baby and the nurse at that moment.** The doctor decided that Sophia needed to go to the newborn ICU right away to have 24-hour monitoring of her breathing.

Amelia recovered normally and stayed in the Tallahassee Memorial Hospital that night. I went back to the apartment in Alumni Village myself and was quite scared even just to think that I could have lost my precious baby that day. Amelia came home after a two-night stay in the hospital, which was the limit the health insurance company allowed. Sophia continued to remain in the ICU for more time until the doctor thought she was safe to be sent home with us. She was required to wear a 24/7 breath monitor for several months because of the breathing problem. **That was a tough period for me as I needed to take care of both Amelia and a newborn with a risk of breathing difficulty**. The monitor's alarm went off several times, and I rushed to adjust Sophia's body to help her breathe. A medical company set up the breathing monitor device. The staff also taught me how to use it myself. I worried about the cost of this device and asked how much it would cost per month to rent it. The staff told me it would be free for us while looking around our poor student apartment. As a poor student family with a newborn, we also received food stamps to cover baby formula, milk, and eggs.

Because there was no help from any family and we had no experience as parents, Amelia and I had to rely on books to raise Sophia along with limited guidance from nurses. We were nervous at every step, especially when Sophia had a breathing problem in the first several months. **Sophia had a dislocated arm when she was about one year old and cried continuously for hours. We brought her to the emergency room and waited long hours before seeing an ER doctor. That doctor took an X-ray and could not fix her arm before we went home. Sophia cried most of the night without getting much sleep.** We took her to see a pediatrician on the 2nd day. It was lucky that the pediatrician knew how to restore her dislocated arm. In several minutes, Sophia was fine and started smiling. Sophia's breathing issue improved a lot after six months, and the doctor said she did not need to wear a monitor device anymore.

Sophia also brought us much joy and happiness as parents, especially me. We had many wonderful moments at home, in the park, and other places. I had been drifting alone for so many years since I was 13 and got used to a bachelor's life, even after marrying Amelia. Sophia's birth gave me a sense of responsibility and ownership as a father to raise and care for her. **I realized that I needed to prepare myself and the whole family well financially to avoid the tough life I had in my childhood for my child.** This included spending only on what was really needed, saving for the future, and preparing for unexpected events and the worst situation by being frugal. In addition, I started to separate myself from others, especially my baby, on the cups, spoons, bowls, and chopsticks I used in order not to bring any germs to them accidentally.

Soon after the birth of Sophia, we bought a better car with a working AC (Air Conditioning) as it could be too hot for the baby in Florida during summer. It was a Buick Regal and cost US$6700.00. It used up all of our multiple-year savings. We drove this car later in the summer of 1997 to move to UIUC for my postdoc job and then to Kansas City in the summer of 1998 to start my first industry job at EM.

Summer 1997, Park in Tallahassee (Sophia and Walter)

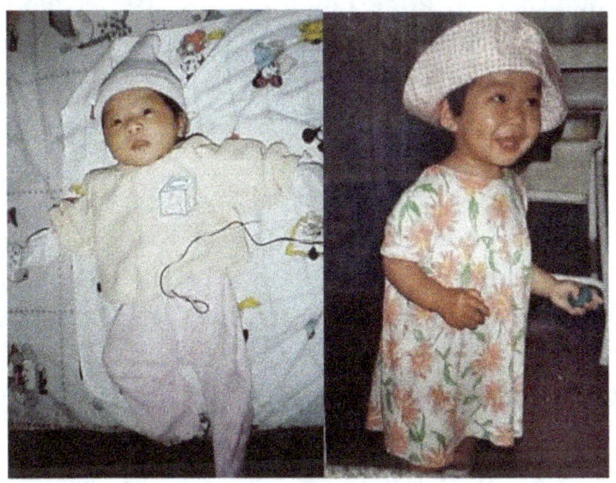

Left: Baby Sophia with Breath Monitor
Right: Baby Sophia in Tallahassee Apartment

12.3.7 Insurance Coverage and Struggle with Medical Expenses

I started to experience and taste the complexities and difficulties of health and auto insurance in Tallahassee. After my emergency visit and multiple night hospitalization in 1994, I received huge medical bills even with coverage of health insurance. An individual is powerless when dealing with big institutions like insurance companies and hospitals. Similarly, Amelia had a car accident in 1994. It was her fault, per the police. The auto insurance would not cover the loss, citing that her name was not shown on the insurance policy even though we had listed her as a family when purchasing the insurance. I had to file a complaint with the Florida State Consumer Department before the insurance company changed its decision and covered the expense.

After Sophia's birth, we had difficulty finding a pediatrician for her because our health insurance was not very good. **At that time, I dreamed that there could be a national universal health program that could provide basic health insurance coverage for its people in the USA, just like in many developing countries and almost all other developed ones**.

12.3.8 Visit to Nearby Cities

We visited several nearby cities in Florida during that period, including Disney in Orlando (Disney and Splendid China), Panama City, St. Augustin, Daytona Beach, Tampa, and Jacksonville. Florida is a good place for a family life, though there is not much industry with engineering jobs. The weather is similar in Fujian and Guangdong. In the summer of 1994, we rented a beach house in Panama Beach with several friends and stayed overnight to enjoy the beautiful beach, ocean, sunrise, and sunset. Before we left Florida for UIUC, we also drove to visit a friend in Tampa, Florida.

12.3.9 Football at Florida State University

I started to watch and like football at FSU as it had one of the best programs in the nation at that time. We went to the FSU football stadium to watch the home game and learn American football rules. Understanding American football was critical to joining American culture. Any home game day became a celebrated holiday in Tallahassee and nearby towns. FSU won a championship in 1994. In the 1990s, Florida had three strong football programs: FSU, the University of Florida, and Miami University. FSU and UF have been rivals, like OSU and Michigan, for many years.

12.3.10 Green Card Application

Between 1996 and 1997, I applied for permanent residence in the USA (a green card) after learning that several friends at the University of Iowa had successfully done that while still doing their Ph.D. By then, I had had several technical publications, including ones in respected international journals. I also obtained several strong recommendation letters from Dean Shen and other scholars. Therefore, the application went well and was approved in early 1997. Amelia and I filed our status adjustments, including physical exams and fingerprints, in Jacksonville before we left Tallahassee for UIUC in 1997. This was very important for a foreign student. Some immigrants took more than ten years to get a green card.

12.3.11 Ph.D. Dissertation Defense and Graduation

May 1997 Outside Our Apartment

May 1997, Ph.D. Dissertation Defense Day with Dean Shen

Left: May 1997 Ph.D. Classmates and Dean Shen
Right: Graduation Day Inside Engineering School.

I finished my Ph.D. research and had a successful dissertation defense in the spring of 1997. The graduation ceremony was held in May 1997, which was a happy moment, as shown in the attached pictures.

12.3.12 Dean C. Shen

Dean Shen was one of the critical people in my life (贵人) as my Ph.D. study advisor. He was the department chairman of Mechanical Engineering at The University of Iowa before 1993 and Dean of FAMU-FSU College of Engineering from 1993 to about 2008. My admittance into the Ph.D. program at The University of Iowa and receipt of full financial assistance in 1991 occurred while he was the department chairman of mechanical engineering. I did not know him, as I was still in Shanghai then. When I was in a difficult position at The University of Iowa in 1993, Dean Shen accepted me as his Ph.D. student so that I could continue my Ph.D. study with his guidance. When I was sick with severe duodenal bleeding, he assured me that I should rest and recover well before going back to regular work as a TA and RA. Dean Shen gave me strong recommendations and full support when I applied for a green card and jobs in the USA. I was happy he visited me in SJTU when I was teaching there in 2004. I learned a lot from him as a teacher, scholar, department chairman, and Dean of the engineering college.

12.3.13 Friends

We met many friends in Tallahassee, including CZ Guo and his wife HX, FJ Shen and his wife ZC, YX Yang and her husband PX, LG, CX Xu and his wife. The parents of FJ helped babysit Sophia when we needed help.

CZ came to FSU to start his graduate study in the civil engineering department with the help of LG and me. We spent several years closely together in Tallahassee before he landed a job in Atlanta. He helped us while I was hospitalized in 1994 and when Sophia was born in 1996.

MS Lin, my cousin back in Lindun, visited Tallahassee around 1996. MS was also SiGe's classmate and close friend from elementary school and high school back in Changtai. I tried to find him an opportunity to study as a graduate student in Tallahassee but did not succeed because of visa issues.

CX Xu and his wife were our neighbors and friends in Alumni Village. Their daughter was at the same age as Sophia. They played together well. We visited them in Tallahassee later in 2016.

12.3.14 Visiting Scholars from China

During our stay in Tallahassee, Dean Shen invited several groups of visiting scholars from China. The first one was from the Tsinghua Hydraulic Engineering department, where I graduated in 1985. Surprisingly, Teacher Bi, who was the head teacher of our class in Tsinghua, was one of them, along with the others. I helped them rent a 3-bedroom apartment in Alumni Village and took them to visit Georgia Tech University and the University of South Florida during their 3-month stay. WH Feng came in 1996, and we became friends. There were also other scholars from other universities. I acted as a coordinator and managed their external activities with the help of others like CZ Guo. During that period, I quietly observed how Dean Shen managed the College of Engineering, especially complicated political and personnel relations, which helped my future professional career in the USA.

12.3.15 Search for a Job

I started looking for a job several months before my Ph.D. graduation. Even though I sent out more than one hundred applications, mostly by mail, but there was little response. Few openings required a Ph.D. degree in my area, especially when the economy was still not good in 1997. I did get an interview with a software company in Boston, which was owned by an MIT mechanical engineering professor. My Ph.D. research direction was mature, so there were almost no openings in US universities in this area. Dean Shen helped me with some funded research work right after my graduation In May 1997 for several weeks with pay. Fortunately, in the summer of 1997, I got an offer from NCSA (National Center for Supercomputing Application) at UIUC for a postdoc research position. We were excited to move again after four years of stay in Tallahassee.

Tallahassee, Florida, is a special place for me and my family. Our daughter, Sophia, was born here. I received my Ph.D. from FSU, and my life journey almost ended in this city.

Chapter 13
Postdoc Research in UIUC from 1997 to 1998

13.1 Travel from Florida State University to UIUC

In the summer of 1997, we mailed out most bulky items, like quilts, to the home of Amelia's cousin, Olivia, in UIUC by the post office before moving. One night before our departure, we had a good dinner at the home of CX Xu, who was still our neighbor in the Alumni Village of FSU. WH Feng was the last to see us off in Tallahassee that morning, as he was still living in Alumni Village. It was a bit emotional that day to leave Tallahassee, and we did not come back as a family to visit until December 2016. By then, I was more confident in long-distance driving as we had driven to Orlando and Tampa. At that time, we had a better car, a Buick Regal, too. To be safe, we stopped every 2 to 3 hours to rest for this car and ourselves. Until now, we have adopted travel principles of leaving early in the morning and arriving at the destination before dark in the evening.

We stopped at CZ Guo's home in Atlanta for two nights and then drove to Paducah, Kentucky, for an overnight stay in a motel. Paducah was a small town in the Midwest with a small population. We were lucky to find a Chinese restaurant and excited to order a duck. When the waitress delivered the duck to us, it was surprising that there was no bone or taste of duck meat. The waitress told us they took out only duck meat, smashed it, and cooked it with a strong, sweet, and sour sauce. Most American customers could not handle meat bone in a dish. In the early morning of the 2nd day, we arrived at Olivia's home and were excited to see them again. Olivia and her husband gave us a warm reception. They even offered us to stay in their master bedroom before we got the rented apartment in UIUC.

With the help of Olivia, we rented and moved into a 2-bedroom apartment for UIUC students with families quickly. The rent was about US$300.00. We quickly bought two mattresses from a yard sale in the apartment compound. We also went to Salvation Army and Goodwill stores to purchase several needed items, including a drawer. This drawer is still used today. The dining table was bought from a yard sale for US$20.00, as the owner was a student from Brazil who needed to move back to his country.

Urbana-Champaign is a small college town like Iowa City, with a population of about 100,000. It is about two-hour drive from Chicago. UIUC has one of the best engineering colleges in the nation, including computer science and mechanical engineering. The campus layout of UIUC is very similar to that of Tsinghua University in Beijing.

13.2 Postdoc Research in NCSA at UIUC

My supervisor was Dr. D Moradi, a Senior Scientist with NCSA (National Center for Supercomputing Application) at UIUC during that period. My research direction was in CFD. I sat in the Beckman Institute at the UIUC campus, which hosted many NCSA research staff. We worked on projects funded by industries through ACRC (Air-Conditioning & Refrigerant Center). The experimental work was done with a professor in the mechanical engineering department. The Internet was in its infancy in 1997. UIUC and NCSA played a role in the development of this new technology. **Many scientists and scholars from different countries worked in NCSA and UIUC, which was the strength of the USA as an immigration country that attracted the brightest people from all around the world. This is one of the key reasons the USA has developed into the dominant power since 1865. In** addition, no war has occurred on this land since then because of its stable political system, which has successfully balanced the interests of conflicting sectors. Any country with enough territory and natural resources, like the USA, can be developed into a major power if it adapts a similar immigration policy to the USA to attract talent worldwide under a balanced, tolerant, and inclusive political system.

13.3 Family and Friends

We had a good time with Olivia's family during our stay at UIUC, including the first Thanksgiving dinner with a delicious turkey. Olivia cooked the turkey well, and we enjoyed that meal very much.

We met several friends at UIUC, including WZ Yin and his wife. In 1997, we visited PH He and his wife in Chicago and stayed in their home for several days. PH He was at the University of Iowa with me in 1992. He worked in Chicago at a corporation while I was at UIUC. BC and his family from Iowa City also joined us.

We first met JD Xu and his wife in Urbana-Champaign. JD was also from Fangyang, a town in Changtai District. His village, Keshan, is only about 8 km from Lindun. In 1998, he was doing his postdoc at Washington University in St. Louis. We went together to visit MJ Yang in Chicago.

Beckman Institute UIUC 1997

Amelia started taking accounting classes at Parkland Community College in 1997 as I had a better income as a postdoctoral research associate. She could not continue teaching English in the US as few job opportunities were available. Accounting was a new major suitable for her. She is still working in accounting now to support the family. Sophia also had a wonderful time in Urbana-Champaign and quality time with Olivia's kids.

13.4 Search for a Job and Episodes during the Interview Trip to Kansas City (KC)

The US economy started recovering in 1998, and some friends found decent jobs in industry. I started looking for an industry job in the spring of 1998 and soon got an interview opportunity with EM Ventilation Product (EV, an EM Corporation division). EM was a Global 500 corporation. The company was located in Kansas City. I needed to fly there from a small airport in Urbana-Champaign to Chicago and then from Chicago to Kansas City. The plane from Urbana-Champaign was quite small, and the weather that day was not good. **In the middle of the flight, the whole plane suddenly dropped substantially. Many passengers screamed and got scared.** I have avoided taking small planes since then.

The plane from Chicago to Kansas City was delayed, and I missed the Limousine EV arranged to pick me up from the airport. Hence, I got to take a taxi to the hotel the company reserved. That was the first time I took a cab in the USA. I found a tip item on the bill when we arrived at the hotel. I asked the taxi driver how much I should give as I never had this kind of tipping experience before with a taxi. The taxi driver said two fifty. I misunderstood that he asked for US$250.00 and told him that was too high. I then gave him about US$23.00 as a tip for a taxi fee of about US$30.00. Someone joked with me later that the driver should say "Merry Christmas" to me for such a high tip I gave him. This was a perfect example of my poor English listening skills in daily conversation, even though I had been in the USA for more than six years with a Ph.D. Since then, I have forced myself to be involved in different kinds of conversations with Americans and watch all kinds of TV shows and movies in English. I have now watched many Western movies and comedies like "Seinfeld," "Becker," and "Big Bang Theory."

The interview went well, and soon after, I received a good offer to be a senior engineer with EM Corporation. I accepted quickly and informed my supervisor in NCSA so we could move soon. Many years later, I realized I might have accepted that offer too quickly because this position might not suit me. I did not quite understand the job market in the US industries at that time. This EV division was small, with only about 200 people and a small engineering team. I could have waited for other opportunities and picked a better one with a bigger engineering development team. A position in a big team could better utilize my wide range of skills and knowledge with an advanced degree.

After officially receiving EV's offer, we returned to Kansas City to look for an apartment. The trip was funded through the offer package on meals and lodging. We found a big apartment complex near EV called Bentley Place at that time and applied for an apartment immediately. There were many buildings inside this Bentley campus housing different kinds of apartments. Luckily, SJ Zeng and his wife had lived in Kansas City after finding a job there in 1998. We got to meet them again over there. I purchased our first brand-new car, a Toyota Camry, during that trip with the help of JS. That new car was parked in the parking lot of their apartment for a while before we officially moved to Kansas City in September 1998. This 1998 Camry was used for 18 years until 2016, when it was traded in.

Chapter 14
Life in Kansas from 1998 to 2005

Moving to Kansas City from Urbana-Champaign was relatively easy as it was a shorter driving distance. We stopped by DJ's home in St. Louis for one night before arriving in Kansas City. After arriving in the early afternoon, we got the apartment keys that day so we could live there that night. It was a spacious two-bedroom apartment with central heating and air conditioning. The living space was about 100 square meters. The rent was more than US$600.00, which I could afford with my income as a senior engineer with EV. Inside the Bentley campus, there were two outdoor swimming pools, several tennis courts, a daycare center, and a good indoor fitness facility, including a table for table tennis. In 2003, before I went back to teach at Shanghai Jiaotong University, we moved to another 2-bedroom apartment in Bentley Place to share with a friend. In 2004, we then moved to a one-bedroom apartment in Charter House, a neighboring apartment complex by Bentley Place.

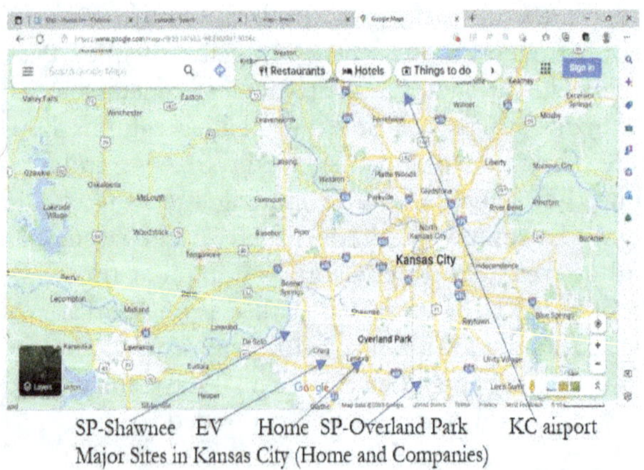

SP-Shawnee   EV   Home SP-Overland Park   KC airport
Major Sites in Kansas City (Home and Companies)

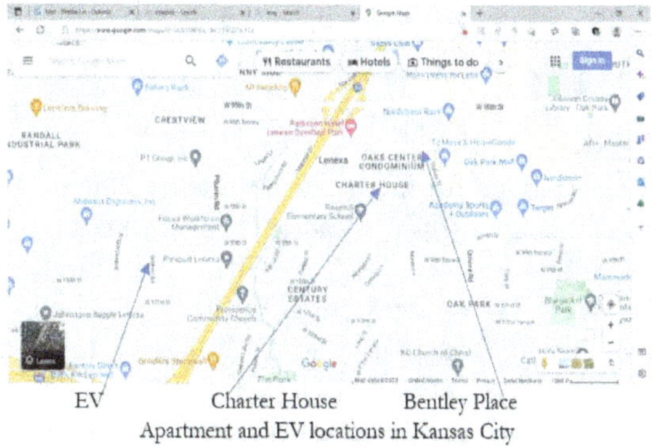

EV   Charter House   Bentley Place

Apartment and EV locations in Kansas City

14.1 Engineer in EM Ventilation Product (EV) at EM

EM has been a global Fortune 500 company for many years. It has been well known on Wall Street for its agile financial management and good performance to its shareholders. It achieved that by constantly buying and selling companies all these years. They acquired profitable businesses aggressively and sold out less outstanding businesses quickly. EV was one of the businesses EM purchased before 1997 and sold out soon after 2003. As a senior engineer in EV, I reported to Vice President of Engineering Richard Taylor. I also worked closely with colleagues like NT Pham and XH He. At that time, EV was a leading manufacturing company for industrial ventilation products like fans and blowers. I was responsible for CFD analysis and development of new products using turbomachinery technology. The working hours were from 7:00 am to 4:00 pm with a one-hour lunch break. I could go home for lunch because it was within a several-minute drive.

On the first day of this job, I was asked to learn to use commercial software for CFD analysis and produce results and reports in a major meeting within five days. That was a low-cost and second-line software with limited CFD and

FEA analysis capacity. NT helped me with how to use that software. I worked hard and produced good reports on time.

It was arranged for me to have some training in the first month, including a trip to Chicago to learn how to use the Pro-E CAD design tool. Jack, an Italian American born and raised in New York City, went with me. I asked him many questions about American culture, including the movie " The Godfather" and the sitcom "Seinfeld." I was surprised to learn about the many differences between American and Chinese cultures. During the trip, I got to see PH He again in Chicago.

The president of EV was young at 32 years old and had an MBA from Northwestern University. This was a common requirement to be an executive in major corporations like EM. He had a BE degree in mechanical engineering. This was a cultural shock as seniority was the key to moving up in China in the 1980s, not degrees like MBAs.

This job in the US manufacturing industry involved people with different backgrounds, from finance, sales, marketing, engineering, procurement, manufacturing, and service. I saw a bigger and more accurate picture of the US than in the universities. Each month, all departments had a major meeting to report their past progress, issues, and next steps. Good speakers could present well on the plan, answer or ask challenging questions, and always stay positive and constructive. Their conversations were often humorous and friendly. They even joked with much slang, which non-native speakers did not easily understand. It seemed that many high school students in the USA got training in public speaking, which helped them a lot in their future careers. In the USA, successful politicians were often excellent public speakers who used those skills to gain support from the public and their constituents. I realized that my English communication skills and my understanding of the US culture needed to be improved. I also had the chance to meet and talk to blue-collar workers who earned much less than the salaried employees. Low-income families in the USA cannot afford a comfortable life. One worker worried about the medical bills from his wife's diabetes and had to continue working in his late 60s. Another colleague had to continue working to keep health insurance for himself and his family with two kids while he was fighting for his life from cancer. A single father at EV in his late 30s needed to work multiple jobs to save enough money for his wedding, which cost him around US$1500.00. They usually had lunch with slices of pizza or a simple sandwich with a soft drink.

14.1.1 Trip to Visit Major Customers in Oklahoma and Texas

In 1998, I visited several customers in Texas and Oklahoma to understand their needs for new products. NT Pham went with me, supported by salespeople in those regions. It was my first time visiting Tulsa, Dallas, Houston, and San Antonio. I was impressed with the River Walk area in San Antonia, where one sales associate took us for dinner.

14.1.2 Trip to White Plains and New York City

In 1999, I had a business trip to White Plains in New York and got to drive to Manhattan to meet MJ Yang and DZ Li. MJ worked at NYCU (New York City University). We had lunch together in Chinatown and saw DZ's apartment near Columbia University. I drove back to White Plains alone in the evening after it got dark through Manhattan, which was challenging but a small accomplishment as there was no GPS then.

14.1.3 Cooperation with the University of Florida on CFD Development

EV had a contract for a research project with Professor SW Huang at the University of Florida (UF) before I joined the company in 1998. I got to continue working with Dr. Bedi and Dr. Martin on the development and visited UF in Gainesville in the spring of 1999. During that trip, I drove back to Tallahassee to see Dean Shen and some old friends there.

14.1.4 Trip to FU in Connecticut and AN in Pittsburgh

I had onsite training on FU (CFD) and AN (FEA) software in the winter of 1998. FU's headquarters was in Hanover, Connecticut. I flew to Manchester in New Hampshire and drove about 2 hours to Hanover in Connecticut. It was very cold in winter, and I had to drive in a winter snowstorm during that trip. Hanover is a small town where Dartmouth College was also located. I did find several Chinese restaurants over there for dinners. During that trip, I started to have a strong allergy to things like dust, mold, and others, which later developed into allergies year-round. I saw Dr. G Sheng and another scientist in FU who got their Ph.D. from FSU.

I met HD Huang and her daughter when I was training in Pittsburgh on AN. HD worked over there in 1998 and nicely showed me the city of Pittsburgh that evening. Pittsburgh is a hilly city, and it is not easy to drive around. In AN, I also met several friends who were also at UIUC doing a postdoc in 1997.

There have been many foreign-born scientists in both FU and AN, the world's leading simulation software companies for CFD and FEA, all these years. This is one of the major reasons the USA maintains its dominant position in technology worldwide. It can attract many talents worldwide to contribute to its development in high-tech areas.

14.1.5 Trip to Beijing in 2000

In 2000, I attended a conference in Beijing and met some classmates and teacher Bi from Tsinghua. There have been many changes in Beijing and Tsinghua since my visit in 1991. During the trip, I started to explore the possibilities of teaching back in China. CY Shen helped me a lot in this exploration.

During my undergraduate study in Tsinghua from 1980 to 1985, none of my family members and relatives ever visited me because we were so poor. I could only go back to see them in Lindun twice during those five years, in 1981 and 1983, respectively. During my trip to Beijing in 2000, I asked SanGe and SiGe to bring my mother to visit Beijing and Tsinghua during my conference trip, which turned out to be a great decision. It was the first time they traveled by airplane and visited Beijing and Tsinghua. They saw the No. 13 dormitory building on the Tsinghua campus where I used to stay. I funded their trips, including air tickets and hotels. We all stayed in a hotel arranged by the conference committee. The buffet-style breakfast included many varieties of healthy and good foods that my family in Lindun had never seen before. I spent the weekend accompanying them to the Great Wall and the Tsinghua campus.

14.1.6 Loss of Passion Due to Limited Opportunities and Slow Business in EV

EV's products were fans and blowers, which were not competitive in the global markets. Its business started to slow down soon after 1999. US and China relations were warming up then, and many USA companies started to source parts and products from China to cut costs. The name of Alibaba began appearing on the internet at that time. I started to sense that EV could not last long and that I needed to find other opportunities later. At the same time, EV did not have enough technology activities as this division was too small. My supervisor and colleagues could see that my passion for work was declining. In April 2001, EV cut its workforce due to slowing business, and I had to leave the company. Amelia was still studying accounting as a full-time student at Johnson Community College. Fortunately, I could find another job in Kansas City within one week, which was important to our family's health insurance. At the same time, we still lived in a rental apartment and had enough savings to last a while. We had been frugal on spending after the previous harsh economic experience in Iowa and Tallahassee. I sent a job application on Saturday and got a phone interview from SP two days later. The onsite interview was conducted on Wednesday of that week, and a job offer was received two days later on Friday. I was able to start working on this new company next Monday. Soon after I left EV, EM sold this division. Almost all of my previous colleagues, including my supervisor in the engineering department, left the company very quickly.

14.2 Engineer in SP and CEO Friend Henry Schmidt

SP was a small telecommunication company owned by investors from New York City and Boston. I was lucky to meet several good colleagues and friends over there. My supervisor, David Brown, VP of engineering, was one of the nicest people I had ever met. He had a BE and MS degree in engineering and had been in the telecommunication industry for over 30 years by 2001. David grew up on a farm in Nebraska and loved watching sports, including football and basketball. He had always behaved like a gentleman and treated others nicely. It was a pleasure for me to work for him. The president and CEO of SP, Henry Schmidt, was a good friend to me. When Amelia's parents visited us, he invited our whole family to have a nice dinner at his home. Henry told me sincerely that my family could come to them for help while I was teaching at SJTU because Amelia and Sophia were still in Kansas City. He also gave me tips on what to wear in business environments in Western countries. Henry kindly reminded me to save enough money on conservative 401K funds by sharing his lessons on retirement investment. He grew up in Germany with an engineering degree and moved to Canada and the USA to work in the telecommunication industry for many years. His wife was a very nice lady from Denmark.

I was hired as a thermal specialist and mechanical engineer to improve the electronic cooling design of the product in SP. My first project was to develop an improved design to lower the interior temperature of the electronic enclosures, which included concept, mechanical design, prototype building, lab testing, and production support in the factory. SolidWorks CAD software was used to design from parts and assembly to the final BOM (Bill of Material). The prototype was built in the SP factory. I conducted lab testing myself. It was verified that the thermal performance met the market requirement by lowering the interior temperature by more than 20 degrees (F). This new design received an invention patent later in the USA.

The SP office was first in Overland Park of Kansas City and moved to Shawnee after 2004. The factory was in another small town of Winsor in Missouri, about a two-hour drive from Overland Park. Winsor had a population of about 1,000. In the 2000s, the average single house in Kansas City cost about US$150k and about US$50k in Winsor. I drove myself several times to this factory by leaving early in the morning from home, working for several hours, and coming home before 6:00 pm. Even though the salary was lower than in Kansas City, people in Winsor's factory lived a happy life. Most of them were nearby farmers. This factory job gave them a 2nd income. One manufacturing engineer told me that he enjoyed life in this small town because most of his family was nearby, and the cost of living was also lower. He built his race car and participated in tournaments frequently. Tim, VP of manufacturing, managed this factory. He had his own small and probably old airplane. He often flew to other cities and states for personal travels. His small plane cost about US$50k. **When we discussed the GDP and family incomes of each state in the USA, they argued that it depended on how you define richness and wealthiness.Many billionaires did not have happy lives as they had only money**.

Most of the SP office employees would go out for lunch every Friday. To fit into this new team and better understand US culture, I joined them almost every week and tried different restaurants with different foods. Gradually, I learned a lot about food and restaurants in the USA, and I could easily understand the menu. Back in 1998, I was arranged by the airline to stay in a hotel during a business trip due to the bad weather. I was with EM then. The airline also provided passengers a food voucher for dinner in the hotel restaurant. I did not understand the menu and ordered a steak without side dishes or vegetables. When the server delivered the bare steak, I had to ask for side dishes before eating. I had eaten mostly Chinese food before, which was not the favorite of most SP colleagues. Many of my SP colleagues lived locally and did not visit foreign countries. There was an annual company picnic and celebration event each year, held in Winsor, where the factory was located. There was a golf course in Winsor. It cost only US$6.00 per 18-hole game then. I played golf on that course for the first time when my supervisor, David, lent me his son's golf clubs.

14.2.1 911 Event and Role Expansion in SP

On the morning of Sept 11, 2001, I was working in the office as usual. Suddenly, someone said there was a bombing of the World Trade Tower in New York City, and minutes later, the 2nd tower was hit. More news came in that evening. This event reshaped US foreign policy dramatically and impacted domestic policy. SP's business was impacted severely. It lost its biggest customer, which accounted for over 50% of sales. Most factory workers and some office employees were laid off. The company badly needed to cut its costs to survive. I was asked to expand my responsibilities to find lower-cost suppliers in China to help SP. I started to travel to China frequently. Eventually, we found good suppliers in Shanghai, Kunshan of Suzhou, and Nanjing. They became stable and reliable suppliers to SP. I also explored and visited other suppliers in Shenzhen, Wuxi, and Wuhu of Anhui. In Nanjing, one of the suppliers treated me with live snake bile with alcohol as an honored guest. Besides quotations of components and estimation of the shipping cost from China to the USA, I also provided technical support on product and manufacturing requirements, as those suppliers were producing the products based on SP's designs.

14.2.2 Trip to China with Board Chairman and CEO

In about 2002, SP board chairman Jeff, one of the major New York City (NYC) investors, wanted to visit suppliers in China. I planned the trip for the group to see major potential suppliers in Shenzhen, Shanghai, Suzhou, Wuxi, Nanjing, and Taizhou Jiangsu. The trip lasted about 12 days for him, CEO Henry, Steve, and me. Steve was the director of the engineering team. Jeff flew separately from NYC, while the rest flew by economy from Kansas City. We met in the Shenzhen hotel first. After the visit, the potential supplier invited us to have a nice meal in a good restaurant. Jeff asked if SP needed to "pay" for this meal treatment. I explained that this was a traditional hospitality any Chinese company would show to their potential customers at the beginning of business talks. In Shanghai, we stayed in the Hilton Hotel in the Jingan District during the trip. The supplier invited us to dinner at a good restaurant by Nanjing Road one night. After dinner, we walked on Nanjing Road and randomly visited stores. Jeff bought a cigar from a fancy store, which cost about 100 yuan, and finished smoking it in about 10 minutes. After returning to the hotel around 10:00 pm, he proposed going to the bar on the top floor of the Hilton hotel for drinks, which cost each of us several hundred yuan again. The night view of downtown Shanghai from the bar was fantastic. The bar was full of businessmen from major global companies who were exchanging experiences doing business in China. After visiting suppliers in Shanghai and Kunshan Suzhou, we needed to see suppliers in Jiangsu. Most of us checked out of the hotel to save the cost and would return later to stay in the same hotel. One night in a Hilton hotel cost more than one month's salary for many workers in China at that time. Jeff did not check out and paid to hold the same room during those nights for convenience. I was surprised by what he was doing. Henry told me that Jeff was an independent rich person in America and could afford to do so.

14.2.3 New CEO and First Wealthy Person I Met Personally

At the beginning of 2005, Henry lost his job as the CEO of SP as the business continued struggling. A new CEO, Paul Weber, was hired. He had been a senior executive of Sprint, a Fortune 500 company in the USA. Paul was the first real wealthy person I met personally. He was president of a major Sprint division for many years, with more than 6,000 employees. When I told him that SP was late paying about half a million US dollars to its suppliers in China, he took out his check and wanted to pay it by himself. CFO Tom stopped him, saying he could not pay company debt using personal money. I thought Paul was just joking until I saw his house. One day, he treated most office people with homemade steak and invited us to his home. When we arrived, we saw a giant mansion with a 6-car garage. The building area was more than 10,000 square feet. It sat at the shore of a major lake with many acres of lot down to the lake water edge. Like a major office building or a theater, the mansion had two tall columns flanking two front doors. In the USA, almost all single-family houses that I had seen had only one front door. His mansion had separate restrooms for men and women. The house was valued at over US$6 million in 2005 in Kansas City, while the average single-family house was valued at US$150k. He did not use credit cards or checks when we had weekly Friday lunch with most office people. Instead, he took out a big stack of US$100 bills and paid in cash. I accompanied him to visit suppliers in China in the spring of 2005. We flew by coach, which I thought would have been challenging for him as SP business did not allow employees to fly business class. During the trip, though, we had a lot of personal talks and got to know each other well, as only the two of us were traveling together. Paul told me he grew up poor in Ohio and did not know how to spend money. His financial agent told him that he needed to spend more and faster. His son had recently opened a startup software company in Chicago, and he invested more than US$30 million in it. He said that he had three good sons. They liked sports and did not do drugs. Paul also told me that he was asked to show how to sell a pen to the hiring manager at his first job interview when he was young in order to demonstrate his customer interaction skills. During the trip, the supplier invited us to have a fancy dinner in an elegant restaurant called DingXian Garden (丁香花园), a former garden house of Li Hongzhang (李鸿章). Li Hongzhang was the premier of the Qing Dynasty around the 1890s. Paul almost ate nothing during that dinner as he was not used to Chinese food and had not had that style of seafood before. After dinner, I saw him eating crackers from Kansas City in the hotel room.

14.3 Son's Birth

Amelia graduated from Johnson Community College with an associate degree in accounting at the end of 2001. She found a full-time job in IB, a Fortune 500 baking company. Our son, Patrick, was born on May 8, 2002. Amelia had only two weeks of paid vacation from the company and applied for four weeks of non-paid maternity leave. She stayed at home for six weeks before returning to work. Amelia's parents came to visit us several months before Patrick was born. They helped us a lot, caring for the baby and Amelia during those months after May 8th, 2002. It was a pity that we could not find much time to bring Amelia's parents to tour the USA because Amelia and I had to work full-time with two young kids. The birth of a son brought us much joy. It also added more responsibilities to my shoulders. The telecommunication industry, including the SP business, continued struggling at that time due to global competition. I needed to find a better opportunity to support my family and give them a better future. In 2002, all signs in the USA pointed to the opportunities in China. I started looking for a teaching position in China, hoping that I would give my family a better life. In addition, I had always wanted to be a professor since I came to the US for my Ph.D. Because I planned to return to teach in China alone in the first semester while Amelia and Sophia remained in the USA, we let Amelia's parents take Patrick back in October 2002 when they returned to Fujian, China. That was a very painful decision for us. Patrick stayed in our hometown until March 2005, when I brought him back to the USA during a business trip.

Happy Family Outside and Inside Apartment in Bentley Place
(Kansas City 2002)

Left: Family in Lindun, China (2003)
Right: Sophia in KC Charter House Apartment (2004)

14.4 Decision to Teach in SJTU

At the end of 2002, I visited several universities in China after a business trip to the SP's suppliers. First, I met the chairman of the mechanical engineering department at Shanghai Jiaotong University (SJTU). I then flew to Beijing to talk to Tsinghua's Dean of Engineering Mechanics School. CY Shen helped me during my job search in China, which I greatly appreciated. He accompanied me to Hefei Anhui for an official interview at the University of Science and Technology of China (USTC). I got an on-site offer from USTC to be a full professor in the Department of Mechanics. Soon after the visits, I also received offers from Tsinghua and SJTU. Eventually, I accepted the offer from SJTU because of several other considerations, such as location and possible funding sources. I started my teaching career in the spring of 2003. PH Huang, CZ Guo, and PW Liu kindly traveled to KC to visit us and stayed in our almost empty apartment before I moved to teach at SJTU. Amelia and Sophia moved into an apartment shared with a friend, which I hoped would be safer for them before I left for Shanghai in 2003. By the end of that year, they moved into a one-bedroom apartment in Charter House, which was by Bentley Place. I visited them about every five months and regularly saw Patrick by returning to Changtai. Those years were hard for me and our families. I swore to myself in 2005 that the whole family would stick together before Sophia and Patrick became adults.

Left: Patrick Lindun Daycare (2004)
Right: My Birthday KC Charter House Apartment (2005)

14.5 Professor at SJTU from 2003 to 2004

As in the US, a professor in a major research university in China must be involved in teaching, research, and service, especially funding search.

14.5.1 Teaching

I enjoyed teaching "Heat Transfer" undergraduate classes for about 60 students. In 2003, all undergraduates at SJTU moved to the Minghan campus, which was about a 45-minute drive from the Xuhui campus. My office was in Xuhui. I needed to take a campus bus several times per week to Minghan to teach that class.Most students were eager to learn, though a small percentage of them were not studying as hard as needed.

14.5.2 Research

I hired one postdoctoral associate who had just finished her Ph.D. from Zhejiang University and three graduate students. As their advisor, I needed to choose research directions for them. More importantly, I needed to find the funded projects and then train them to conduct the research. It was much harder than I expected to get the funded projects. One of the reasons was the lack of a good understanding of social relations and how the system worked in China. I did get a small amount of funding from MA. That was one of the reasons I chose SJTU in 2003, as it was close to MA. I also tried to engage in various activities organized by SJTU to see if there were opportunities to get any funding from some companies. One of them was a major washing machine company in Shanghai. I was also involved in consulting and service work, which might help me fit quickly into society. One major company in Shengzhen invited me to train their engineers in thermal management for two days. I talked continuously for more than 8 hours daily to a large group of engineers for the first time. I got a chance to tour a blower company in Yuxing, Jiangsu. SP also needed my support as I was close to their suppliers. Sometimes, I had to visit those suppliers during the weekend.

14.5.3 Trips and Episode in SJTU

In the winter of 2003, I attended a technical conference in Xian and stayed in a hotel in the Huaqingchi area. It was told that President Jiang Jieshi stayed in this hotel in 1938 when the Xian Event occurred. Two of his generals arrested him to persuade him to stop the civil war so that all forces could fight against the invasion of Japan. I got to visit the

Terra Cotta Warrior Museum during the trip. There were many small souvenir sellers near the gate area. One seller approached me and asked if I was interested in a box of terra cotta statues. When I asked how much it cost per box, he started with 100 yuan. I said "no" and walked away. He followed me and continuously lowered the price by almost 20% per step I walked until it hit as low as 20 yuan. I stopped and bought several boxes of them at that price.

In the spring of 2004, the School of Mechanical Engineering at SJTU arranged a group vacation trip to Nanxin Old Town (南浔古镇) in Huzhou Zhejiang for all faculties and staff. We stayed in nice hotels and had good meals arranged and paid for by the school. I got to see the old elegant house of Shen Wanshan (沈万山), the richest person in the early Ming Dynasty under emperor Zhu Yuanzhang (朱元璋).

One day, in the SJTU campus cafeteria, I met a young person who wore a small, dirty backpack and looked strange. I talked to him and found out he was not a student of SJTU. He told me he was from a nearby province and loved to hang around the SJTU campus. He even attended lectures in some classes without permission. He said that he had been mistreated by campus gate guards several times because he was not an SJTU student. They put him on the floor like a criminal. I bought him a big lunch from the cafeteria and asked him to try again to get into any colleges by attending Gaokao, which he had probably failed several times. He was obviously poor and probably dreamed of being one of these college students on the SJTU campus. He might be looking for leftovers in the cafeteria on that day.

14.5.4 Apartments near SJTU

In 2003, I rented a two-bedroom apartment by Leshan Road and Guangyuan Road near the Xuhui campus of

SJTU. The apartment was in a tall apartment building complex of about 15 stories. I used to exercise by climbing the stairs up and down before dinner, as there was little open space for jogging in Shanghai's downtown area. In the 2nd year of 2004, I rented a one-bedroom apartment on Xinghua Road, which was also close to the SJTU campus.

14.5.5 Dean Shen's Visit to Shanghai

Dean Shen made an official academic visit to SJTU in 2004, giving a seminar on his research hosted by the School of Mechanical Engineering. We had dinner with the vice president of SJTU that day. On the 2nd day, SJTU arranged a car to take Dean Shen and me to tour Zhou Zhuan, an old town (周庄古镇) near Shanghai. Dean Shen and I had lunch inside that old town. After returning to SJTU that day, the driver, a salaried staff in the SJTU transport department, suddenly asked me to give him 50 Yuan for the lunch fee, which surprised me. I checked with the school secretary and was told I did not have to do that. I also took Dean Shen to tour Shanghai's major downtown area. A knee injury was bothering Dean Shen. At that time, he was still working as Dean of Engineering College at FSU even though he was close to 70.

14.5.6 New Friends and Colleagues in Shanghai from 2003 to 2004

During my teaching career at SJTU, I met several good friends and colleagues, including HZ Duang and HG Guo. I appreciated their help during that period. I also got a chance to meet old friends and colleagues in Shanghai, including Teacher Zheng, his family, LD Wen, GA Ye, BG Meng, and KX Zhang et al. KX was my Tsinghua classmate, and he moved to Shanghai from Henan Province to give his son better education opportunities. He had a very good job in Henan, but there were few chances for high school graduates to enter a good university in his hometown province. We bought an apartment in Minghang by the SJTU campus in 2003. Amelia and Sophia visited that apartment in the summer of 2003, as well as the elementary school for the children of SJTU's teachers.

SJTU Colleagues, Postdoc and Graduate Students 2004

14.5.7 Difficult Decision to Resign from SJTU and Return to SP

I resigned from SJTU at the beginning of 2005 due to several considerations. Amelia had difficulty finding office jobs in Shanghai at that age because most positions required candidates under 35. Sophia and Patrick would have a difficult time in the future coming back to the USA to study. With my income in Shanghai, we couldn't afford to send them to international schools in Shanghai, which were as expensive as private schools in the USA. I also could not get used to the new social environment well, as much had changed since 1992. One close friend in Shanghai told me candidly that I should look for chances to make more money. An SJTU colleague who just returned from the USA to teach in the pharmacy school said that I should stay in the USA with such young kids. He came back because his son had already attended college. At the annual physical exam of 2004 in SJTU, I was surprised to find that I had an active Hepatitis B virus. That explained why I frequently got sick with cold and fever during that period. That was the time I found out that I carried the Hepatitis virus from birth, as there was no vaccine in 1965. After my resignation in 2005, HZ Duang kindly took over my graduate students and postdocs and made a good arrangement for them. My postdoc, HG Guo, helped me process the remaining paperwork at SJTU. She was later able to become a faculty member at SJTU. GA Ye later helped us sell that apartment in Minghang. SP company was kind enough to let me return to work for them. The decision to return to the USA was right for the kids and their educational journeys. Sophia got a national finalist scholarship in 2014 to attend Ohio State University (OSU) for her undergraduate degree. She was admitted to UPMC (University of Pittsburgh Medical School) in 2018 after graduating from OSU in the same year. Patrick later matriculated to the Fisher College of Business at OSU (Ohio State University) in 2020 and graduated in May 2024.

14.6 Friends in Kansas City

We had several friends in KC, including SJ Zeng and his wife, SJ Shen and his wife, ZG Shen and his wife, GP Li and his wife, XH He and his wife, and YX Xu and his wife. Both SJ Zeng and SJ Shen studied and got degrees from Fujian Normal University and the University of Iowa. We regularly got together to have a party with all our children. Usually, we had dinner first and then played card games like 120 points with three decks of cards. The children had much fun playing together, too. Each family would bring one to two dishes to the host family. We lived in an apartment in KC, and it was a bit crowded to host so many people. Other families had moved into spacious single houses, making hosting a big party easier. When Amelia's parents visited us, they also attended those parties and enjoyed being with those friends and families. There were several Asian grocery stores in KC, so we got to eat some good Chinese food during those years.

KJ Gao, a friend we met in Iowa, visited us in KC once during a business trip. We also visited his family in Omaha, Nebraska. He had a wonderful wife and two sons. His family also visited us in Columbus, Ohio, later.

14.7 Vacations and Tourist Visits

14.7.1 Camping Trip to Yellow Stone National Park in The Summer of 1999

We met YX Xu and his family in Kansas City and learned that he also graduated from Tsinghua and worked at UIUC as a postdoc. YX was passionate about camping and invited us on a camping trip to Yellowstone. He booked the campsite several months before the summer of 1999. We practiced camping in a state park near Kansas City one weekend to ensure we did not miss any important items. Yellowstone was a two-day drive away from Kansas City. We rented a van for both families and stayed overnight in one small town between Nebraska and Wyoming on the first day. There were only a few hundred residents in that town, with one street, hotel, bank, restaurant, post office, and grocery store to serve nearby residents. Yellowstone was great, as expected. It was hot at 90 F during the day and cold at 30 F at night. Fortunately, we brought enough clothes. YX did good homework on the sites to visit and what to prepare for the camping. We enjoyed the trip with his family a lot. Sophia and YX's daughter played well together as well. No food and drinks were allowed inside the tent to avoid bears coming in to search for food. Driving along the northern part of Yellowstone was challenging and scary as the narrow road had a deep cliff on the side. I probably would not drive that kind of road again. On the way home, we stopped overnight at Cheyenne and had dinner in a Chinese restaurant in this small town.

14.7.2 First Trip to Visit Family in China after Eight Years in The USA during Christmas of 2000

Amelia and I received our green cards in 1999. We visited our family and friends in China at the end of 1999. After so many years of separation from our families, that was an emotional trip. We traveled back to Xiamen through Shanghai. Both sides of the family, including my mother and Amelia's parents, welcomed us at Xiamen airport even though we arrived late at night, about 10:00 pm. I burst into tears when I saw my aged mother. We stayed in Lindun for several days before going to Yanxi to stay with Amelia's parents for a few more days. One day in Lindun, we visited my father's grave in the nearby hills with SanGe and SiGe. Later, we visited XiangChen and stayed at ErGe's home for a few more days. Our high school classmates held a big welcome party for us during our visit to Xiancheng. I was excited to see them again since I had not seen many since our graduation in 1980. They were HL Liu, GZ Xie, SY Xue, JY He, FY Liang, GQ Ye, SY Dai, et al. Changtai No. 1 High School also invited me to talk to their senior high school students, which could motivate them to do well in the coming GaoKao. I was happy to see this campus again after 20 years.

Left: Family Picture at Lindun's New House 1999
Right: Family in Father's Grave 1999

On the way back to the USA, we stopped in Shanghai for a few days and stayed at Teacher Zheng's home. I was excited to meet Teacher Zheng, his family, and colleagues in MA.

14.7.3 Trip to Dallas and Houston during Christmas of 2000

We took a trip to visit Dallas and Houston during Christmas of 2000. We first drove to Dallas to stay in FJ Shen's rental place and then went to Houston while staying at his home. Houston had a big Chinatown full of good restaurants and grocery stores. Seeing FJ's wife, YX Yang, PX, and FS Zhuang again in Houston was nice.

14.7.4 Visit to St. Louis and Chicago with Amelia's Parents in 2002

At the beginning of 2002, before the birth of Patrick, I took a vacation to take Amelia's parents to visit St. Louis and Chicago. Amelia could not go because she did not have enough vacation days saved. We were planning to save her vacation for her rest after the birth of our son. Sophia went with us. We stayed at Tina Xu's home in St. Louis. She and her husband were very hospitable. Both had studied and got their Ph.D. degrees at the University of Iowa. Tina also came from Zhangzhou and graduated from Fujian Normal University. I had a strong headache during the trip because I could not sleep well at night before leaving KC. After St. Louis, I drove to Chicago and stayed at the home of SJ, who was my Tsinghua classmate. We had not seen each other since graduation in 1985. SJ and his family were nice and welcoming to our visit. His older daughter was adorable and played well with Sophia. I felt exhausted at the end of the trip after driving more than eight hours from Chicago back to KC during a snowstorm.

14.8 Amelia's Driving Accident in Kansas City in 2005

Amelia changed the job in 2004 because her previous

company (IB) went bankrupt. The new company was about 20 miles away from home. She needed to drive on Highway 435 to get to the new company. One morning in early spring of 2005, I received a call saying Amelia had a big car accident. I drove to the place quickly and found her car sliding into a deep ditch by Highway 435. Luckily, she was safe. The car was more than 50 meters away from the road. It was snowing that morning, and the road was slippery. Amelia drove too close to the edge of the road, and the car slid into the ditch. The ditch had about a 45-degree slope and was more than 70 meters long. Fortunately, the car did not flip, which would have been a disaster for Amelia. Instead, it stopped in the middle of the slope around 50 meters from the road by hitting a small bump. Amelia said she pushed the brake very hard during the accident, which also helped slow the car down. I called AAA, and they sent a tow truck with a long metal rope. I sat in and maneuvered the car while the AAA truck pulled up our car slowly with that big metal rope. There was no damage to our car. We drove home after the accident. I felt scared after coming home. Amelia's life could be at risk if the car flipped into such a deep ditch. At that moment, I decided we needed to find better jobs elsewhere, so Amelia would no longer have to work in this location.

14.9 Search for Other Opportunities

I returned to work for SP Corporation at the beginning of 2005 after resigning from SJTU. Henry Schmidt was removed from the CEO position soon after I returned as SP's business continued struggling. New CEO Paul Weber joined later, and I accompanied him to visit suppliers in China in March 2005. After the business trip, I returned to Lindun to bring my son back to the USA. Patrick could only speak the Mingnan dialect then and could not communicate with Sophia well. In April 2005, Amelia needed to take a three-day business trip to South Carolina. I had to work full-time while caring for Sophia and Patrick during those days.

Sophia was attending elementary school while Patrick was sent to daycare full-time. **When I saw both children playing around in this tiny one-bedroom apartment, I felt the urge to find a better job to give them a better life environment.**

I started looking for other better opportunities at the beginning of 2005. In early March 2005, I got an interview invitation from Siem in Philadelphia. Siem was a global 100 corporation headquartered in Germany. I needed to fly to Philadelphia for the interview on the first day of daylight saving. **I got sick with a fever, probably due to the active Hepatitis B virus. That morning, I forgot to adjust the clock hour and overslept. When I rushed to KC airport, my flight had already left. That was the only time I missed a flight due to my fault.** I called Siem right away and have not received any responses since then. Later in May, I got an interview with TRAN in Taylor, Texas. TRAN has been one of the leading HVAC companies in the world and had a facility in Taylor at that time. I was interviewed for a senior position in their engineering team. The engineering manager was close to retirement. He and HR told me they were looking for a candidate who could succeed him. That was why I had a group interview with the whole engineering team and answered questions from each of them within 2 hours. The interview went well, and I quickly received a very good offer. However, I did not accept the offer immediately based on my experience in 1997 when I received the offer from EM. **Though the prospect of leading an engineering team of about 12 engineers from different ethnic backgrounds looked appealing, I did not like that Taylor was a very small town of about 10,000 people near Austin.** How long could the facility last under TRAN? Eventually, I turned down the offer and continued the search for other opportunities. My decision was correct, as TRAN shut down that facility several years later and moved it to Mexico.

Soon, I got an interview opportunity from YO International at their headquarters in York, Pennsylvania. YO International was another leading global HVAC company. There were several hundred engineers in this location alone. I was lucky to meet my future managers, Dr. Ryan Meyer, the director of the advanced development center, and Dr. M Gupta, the manager of the heat transfer team. The interview went well, and I received a good offer quickly.

Chapter 15
Engineer in Pennsylvania from 2005 to 2006

15.1 Mysterious Phone Ring and Travel from Kansas City to York

My offer package included a generous relocation package. We sold the old car and shipped the 1998 Camry and other key items. **Before we left that one-bedroom apartment in Charter House, I heard a loud phone ring inside the apartment right before I closed the door, even though the phone and phone line had been disconnected, packed, and shipped one day before. This was the first time I experienced this kind of supernatural phenomenon.** That magical spirit probably was trying to say goodbye to our family after more than one year of stay there. It had been watching and protecting my family during our stay in that apartment.

We stayed in a hotel near KC airport that night while having a good dinner at the home of SJ Shen, which was very close to the hotel. The whole family flew to York through Atlanta airport. CZ Guo worked in that airport, so we got to see him and had a quick lunch together inside the airport. We first had a rental car in York before buying our 2nd new car, a 2005 Honda Accord in York. The company also paid the first six months' rent, so we stayed near the company in a spacious 2-bedroom apartment on Carnegie Road.

15.2 York Pennsylvania

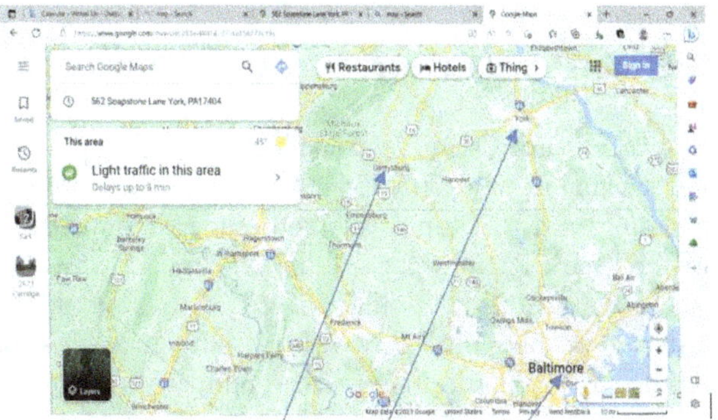

Locations of Gettysburg, York, and Baltimore

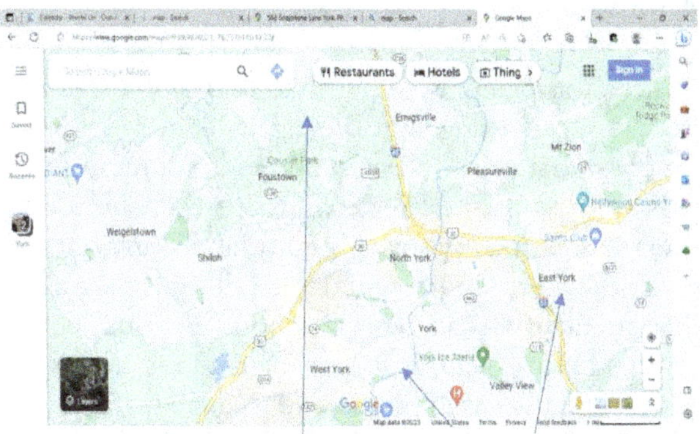

Map of York, PA (Soapstone House, YO JC, Carnegie Apt.)

York had a population of about 200,000 at that time and is about 45 minutes north of Baltimore, Maryland. The local people here differed from those in larger cities such as KC and college towns such as UIUC. Some people who worked in Baltimore and even Washington DC lived in York to avoid the high costs of rents and houses. There were few Asians and Chinese in this city at that time. We needed to go to the nearby town of Lancaster to shop in a small Chinese store, as there was none in York. We built and lived in a house on Soapstone Lane between the end of 2005 and the end of 2006, which might be a mistake as it ended up being difficult to sell in 2007.

15.3 Professional Career

I worked in YO International's advanced department center starting in July 2005. Ryan Meyer was the director of this center, and M Gupta was the manager of the Heat Transfer Team. This was a good time for me to learn about the HVAC (Heating, Ventilation, and Air Conditioning) industry. I pushed myself to learn as much as possible, including going to the office every Sunday to learn new knowledge.

15.4 Family Life

Amelia was planning to return to school to finish her BS degree in accounting but changed her decision after discovering that YO College required accounting students to pass science classes like biology. Instead, she found an accounting job in Gettysburg County, about an hour's drive from York. Patrick was sent to a full-time daycare, and Sophia attended an elementary school in York. That was one of the busiest periods for Amelia and me. Amelia even forgot to refill the gas in the car and told me that the vehicle could not be started because there was almost no gas in the car tank. I called AAA to ask for help, saying my car could not be started because I forgot to put it in the parking position. Sophia did extremely well in school and was asked to test her IQ. The test proved that she should be listed as a talented student with a special curriculum.

15.5 Customized House Building in York

Left: York House (Built in 2006)
Right: York Daycare (2006)

We started to look for a house soon after moving to York, probably because I was too eager to give my family a better living environment. Unfortunately, the house price was higher than our budget in the neighboring areas of South York, which is closer to Baltimore. One colleague and friend, ZL Wen, just built a customized house in the North York area. We decided to do the same and order one in that area. Building or ordering a customized house was quite challenging for us as we never lived in a house before and did not know what was important for a house, including the complicated professional building terminology. I needed to learn quickly and order the right combination of different features and options by understanding many pages of drawings and documents. We also drove to the central York area for several hours to sign the agreement with the builder and the design architecture. It took several months for the builder to break the ground, build, and decorate the house. I needed to drive frequently to the site to watch closely the progress. The house building was finished in the spring of 2006. The builder planted grass seeds for front and back yards to establish the lawn. One day, after a big storm, I found the basement full of water, almost half a meter deep. I called the builder and asked them to check and fix the water leakage in the basement before we could move in. The builder found the issue, rebuilt the foundation for the basement, and finally sealed the water leaking. I purchased a powerful dehumidifier to remove the remaining moisture in the basement by running it continuously for several days. One day before we moved in, I bought a metal mailbox with a long wood pole from Home Depot. It was snowing lightly that day. I dug a deep hole in the ground in the front of the house and installed this mailbox with that long pole. We happily moved into this new house later with the help of several local friends and colleagues. I rented a U-Haul to move some furniture I purchased, including a big sleeping sofa. It was the first time I drove a U-Haul truck.

15.6 Visits to Neighboring Cities

We visited NYC in the summer of 2005 while staying at MJ Yang's home in New Jersey. MJ's parents were with them at that time. It was the first time Amelia, Sophia, and Patrick visited NYC (the Big Apple). MJ was nice to accompany us to tour major sites in NYC, including the Wall Street, 911 site, and Ellis Island. In the winter of 2005, my company, YO, arranged a one-day trip to NYC. We joined the family of ZL Wen to see some other sites, such as Chinatown and Rockefeller Center.

Left: Manhattan NYC (2005)
Right: Wallstreet NYC (2005)

We visited Niagara Falls in the fall of 2005 while staying at the home of PW Liu in Horseheads, New York. We went to Canada's side to see the Fall, and that was the first and the only time we set foot on the land of Canada before 2023.

On the way back to York, we also visited the town where the well-known global company Corning was located.

In the winter of 2005, DZ Li's family and ours booked two rooms in a beach house in Ocean City, Delaware. We spent two nights over there and toured the nearby area. It was nice to catch up with them. DZ had a lovely daughter who was slightly younger than Patrick. We also stayed at their home in New Jersey in the spring of 2006 and visited a theme park nearby.

In the late spring of 2006, we took a one-day trip to visit DC, which was the first time for our family. I was quite impressed at the magnificence of the Mall and the massive buildings around it. Hersey Park is about one hour away from York, and we visited it on a one-day weekend. Right before we left York for Columbus, we visited Baltimore and loved the Inner Harbor.

15.7 Emergency Hospital Visit Due to Kidney Stone Pain

One day in the fall of 2006, I had severe pain in my back in the office, and I went to the emergency room at York Hospital. After a series of examinations, including blood tests and CT, I was told that there was a sizable kidney stone in the ureter close to the bladder. The doctor asked me to drink a lot of water and jump frequently in the next several days. The kidney stone eventually came out with urine. It was close to 4 mm long. I took it to a urologist to test its chemical ingredients. After the test, I was advised to drink plenty of water daily and minimize foods such as tomatoes, tofu, chocolate, spinach, raisins, and strong tea. Since then, I have been found to have kidney stones several times from annual physical exams, even though I have been doing my best to follow the above advice from physicians.

15.8 Looking for Other Opportunities

In the summer of 2006, YO International was sold to JC, which was bad news to many YO employees, including me. JC incorporated YO International with one of its divisions and formed a big division of about 50,000 employees. There was a major reorganization, including YO's advanced development center. My managers left, which was not a good sign for our team. I was still under a one-year agreement with YO to not move due to the relocation package, and I could only wait. In October 2006, YO dissolved its advanced development center, and I was one of many people who needed to leave. I expected this and started sending out my resume. Surprisingly, I got many good responses quickly. In three weeks, I got five personal interviews with well-known global corporations and received three good official offers, including one from LE EM in the 6th week. After careful consideration, I chose to go to LE EM corporation in Columbus, Ohio, reporting to Ryan Meyer, who had just left YO JC to become the vice president of the engineering department in LE.

Chapter 16
Life in Columbus from 2006 to Present

16.1 Move from York to Columbus

I started working in LE EM on Nov 11, 2006, while Amelia and the kids stayed in York. During the Christmas period of 2006, I drove back to York. The move from York to Columbus was a bit complicated as we had a house then. We used the same agent who helped us relocate from KC to York to sell our house. The relocation package from LE EM was good, too, including up to six months' rent in an apartment and some grocery expense reimbursement. After the moving company packed and moved away most of our heavy items, including some furniture, we drove two cars full of important and smaller items from York to Columbus. Sophia and Patrick sat in the old Camry with me while Amelia drove the new Honda Accord alone. It took almost 7 hours to drive, which was the longest one Amelia had ever driven on her own. We stayed in a hotel with a small kitchen near the company for several days before moving into a 3-bedroom apartment in the Polaris area. After staying in that apartment for almost six months, we bought and moved into a house in Dublin, Ohio, in July 2007.

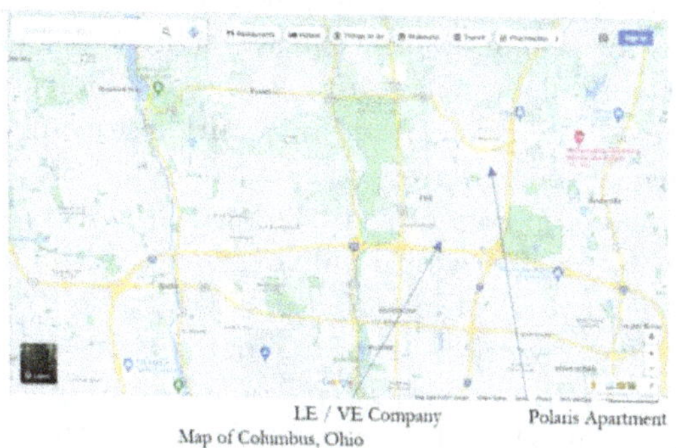

Map of Columbus, Ohio

16.2 Columbus Ohio

Columbus is the capital of Ohio and has a population of about 1.5 million in its metropolitan area. It is one of the fastest-growing cities in the USA. Dublin has been ranked as one of the best cities in the nation for a family to live in. There are several major universities in Columbus, including OSU, Capital University, and Otterbein University, with a large population of Asian and Chinese people. This is probably the best city among the six we have lived in the USA since 1992. Dublin is a suburb of metropolitan Columbus and is a wonderful place for a family with kids. Sophia and Patrick love this place and consider it their home.

16.3 Professional Career

I started working at LE of EM NP on November 11, 2006. I was supposed to have an orientation by HR on the morning of that day to fill out all forms and get to know my working environment. Instead, I joined a global meeting on a global project I would lead. Team members from Europe, China, and Australia traveled to Columbus for a one-week global meeting to kick off this global project.

16.3.1 Corporation of EM and LE

LE in EM NP has been the global leader in cooling and power management of data center equipment, cooling, and control, with its headquarters in Columbus, Ohio. LE has been the #1 brand worldwide in this field for many years. I was excited about the opportunity to work here. EM, a Global 500 corporation, had five business divisions then, with about 150,000 global employees. It had more than 30,000 employees in China alone in 2007. EM NP was one of the five divisions. It had about 20,000 employees worldwide, with its headquarters in Columbus, Ohio. EM NP had an annual revenue of five billion US dollars in 2007.

LE was a subdivision of EM NP. EM NP had about 6,000 employees in China at that time, and its China division headquarters were in Shenzhen. SM Wilson, the boss of Ryan Meyer, was the GM (General Manager) who oversaw LE's global thermal cooling business. There were multiple global projects involving divisions of America, Asia, China, and Europe. The global project I led involved a group of engineers in Xian and Shenzhen. I had to visit them multiple times per year since then.

When I flew to visit China or Europe, the company arranged business or first-class seats. That was the first time I had had such an expensive trip. A business seat usually costs five times more than a coach one. A first-class seat could cost up to eight times more than a coach. At the time, I was also leading another global team with team members from the USA and Europe to develop a tool for marketing and sales to sell our cooling product, which turned out to be an important and politically challenging program until I resigned from the company in 2021.

16.3.2 Visits to Europe

I had visited the team in Slovakia twice before 2016. I flew through Germany for the first time and arrived in Vienna with colleagues. We had a short stay in Vienna's downtown area and had lunch over there. Vienna's buildings looked impressive as the capital of the previous mighty Austria-Hungary empire. The lunch was very salty, similar to what we experienced in Slovakia. We rented a car and drove for about 2 hours to reach Trencin in Slovakia. EM had a big facility in Nove Mesto, Slovakia. We stayed in the nearby city of Trencin. Trencin is a small and beautiful town of about 50,000 people. It had a big historical castle dated for more than 1000 years. There was a guide who explained the history of this castle to us. This guide was very proud of his country's cultural history. When the Mongolian army attacked Vienna and nearby cities 800 years ago, this castle was under siege for a long time. There were still big pits and holes on the wall of this castle left by the big stones thrown by the Mongolian army. On my 2nd trip to Europe, I got a chance to meet FY Xie in London. FY was my Tsinghua classmate and roommate. I toured London's downtown area for only one day while staying in a hotel by the airport. London was a metropolitan as I expected, as the capital of an empire that had dominated the world for over 200 years before 1940. I did not have time to visit the well-known British Museum, which still housed many invaluable historical items worldwide, including those from Greece, Egypt, India, and China. Similar to many major powers in human history, the British Empire had shrewdly controlled most of the world by dividing and manipulating rivals in their territories to fight each other so they could dominate. For example, they controlled the South Asia region, including India, Pakistan, and Bangladesh, with a small army by letting sectors of the Hindu and Muslim populations fight each other. This way, both sides had to seek help from the British. British also forced the sale of opium drugs to China in the middle of the 19th century, which pretty much destroyed a whole generation of the population.

I tried having dinner in the London hotel restaurant and found all the dishes were spicy. When I asked if I could have a non-spicy dish, I was told no, as their food had to be prepared with spicy ingredients.

The EM's cafeteria in Nove Mesto was impressive. Due to the company's subsidies, employees could have a nice lunch with several dishes, including main, side, dessert, and drink, for about 2 Eurodollars. I enjoyed my meal in that cafeteria.

Overall, the cost of living in Europe was much higher than that in the USA, with lower incomes, probably because of higher population density, smaller land areas, and fewer natural resources. However, the health care system in the whole European Union is much better than the one in the USA.

16.3.3 Visit to Mexico

I had a business trip in 2015 to EM's Reynosa factory in Mexico. Reynosa is a city in Mexico bordering a neighboring town of McAllen in Texas. There was much violence in Reynosa at that time due to drug mafia fights. The company required us to stay in a hotel on the Texas side at night. We went to visit the Reynosa factory during the daytime for safety reasons. We traveled in a company vehicle accompanied by a local employee from Mexico. There were many army soldiers with automatic weapons in the customs and on the roads to our factory inside Mexico. The factory was surrounded by a tall wall with an electric fence on top of the wall to protect the employees. We are told not to travel alone inside Mexico. Some of my Columbus colleagues said they heard loud gunfire noises when they were there before my visit. The drug mafia violence brought a lot of harm and damage to the public in Mexico. An EM engineer in Mexico said that the key was the strong demand for drugs from the US market. Those drugs were smuggled from other countries to the USA through the border of the US and Mexico. Mexico's economy was heavily dependent on exports to the USA. It would be a disaster to both the economy of Mexico and the USA if the border were shut down. During the visit, I tasted the authentic Mexican taco, which was soft and delicious, in the factory's cafeteria.

16.3.4 Visit to Thailand and Ride in a Bullet-Proof Limousine

In April 2015, I took a business trip to Thailand to visit a potential supplier located in Bangkok. The hotel I stayed in was decent and close to the airport. It was surrounded by farmland and many poor farmers' houses. In the early morning of the 2nd day, I was picked up and visited the company. We got to travel through a large farming land. The road conditions close to the company were quite poor, with many bumps near the supplier. When we reached the destination, a larger seven-story building appeared before us, which hosted the factory, labs, and offices of this family-owned company. The top story was a living place for the owner's family. There were over 500 employees on this site. The owner was a 2nd generation Chinese man in his late 60s and semi-retired. He spoke very good Chinese with me as he had attended a Chinese school in Thailand before the 1960s. His father migrated to Thailand from Guangdong Maoming in the 1930s. The owner had a Ph.D. in engineering from Thailand and built this company himself from scratch. His son, in his early 30s, was running the company then. Family members of the owner, like his cousin and nephew, occupied most key positions. He also had a manufacturing company in Shanghai since the early 1980s and was planning to close it as the cost of living there had risen significantly. After the business meeting in the morning, he took me to lunch in an exclusive clubhouse inside a fancy golf course. We rode in his pro-long bullet-proof limousine with a dedicated chauffeur. The vehicle was custom-built in Germany. There was an adjustable sealing wall between the chauffeur and the passenger side, which could prevent the chauffeur from hearing any conversation among passengers. A landline phone was available from the passenger seat on the last row to talk to the chauffeur. The clubhouse was for the elite in Bangkok only, with a high membership fee. The owner's son took me for dinner, and we had a long chat about Thailand and the Chinese people there. I visited the Thailand Royal Palace myself on 2nd day before heading back to the USA. Almost all the food there was spicy, including the ones in the hotel.

Chinese people in Thailand have much higher political and social status than those in other Southeast Asia countries. Starting in the early Ming Dynasty of the 1300s under Emperor MingChengzu Zhuli, many people from

Fujian and Guangdong areas moved to southeast Asian countries to escape war and poverty. More than 40% of Thailand's population has a certain percentage of Chinese blood, including that of the King. The owner of the above company and Thaksin Shinawatra, the prime minister of Thailand from 2001 to 2006, were in the same association of Fellow Townpeople (同乡会) as both have the same Chinese last name from Guangdong Province. During the Cold War, from the 1960s to the 1980s, Chinese schools were shut down by governments in almost all Southeast Asian countries, including Thailand. Chinese people were forced to give up their Chinese names and change to local country names. Hundreds of thousands of Chinese were murdered in 1966 in Indonesia. Many were forced to leave even though their ancestors had lived there for generations since the 1700s. I had personally met some of them in China before 1990, including one of my teachers at Tsinghua University. Chinese people in some Southeast Asian countries are still discriminated against in many aspects of their lives, including equal opportunities in education, government jobs, free movement in their own countries, political rights, legal status, and cultural inheritance. They are economic giants and political dwarfs over there.

16.3.5 Manager Change in 2013

In 2013, a major leadership change occurred in LE EM Network Power. The business leader of EM NP retired, and Bob from EM Climate Technology took the position. Soon, Joseph Koch from Copeland, a division of EM Climate Technology, became GM (General Manager) to lead the global thermal cooling business. Ryan Meyer moved to another VP position inside LE. A new VP of engineering, Dr. Larry Weber, was hired from TRAN. Larry was a nice guy with a height of 6'10" (2.08 meters). I accompanied him to visit teams in Shenzhen and Xian, including the Terra Cota Warrior Museum site. Executive management style changed a lot since 2013. I had to cope with the change like other managers. I led another new product development program with a global team in Columbus, Xian, and Shenzhen. This team involved design, testing in the lab and field, product release into production, and sales and marketing service support. The project went well, and I enjoyed it very much.

16.3.6 Three-Year MBA Style Intensive Training in a Leadership Program

Sometime in 2013, I was surprised to receive a notice from HR that I had been selected into a leadership program at EM NP. There were 21 people in this three-year intensive MBA-style program sponsored by the leader of EM NP. Ryan Meyer was likely the one who recommended me to this program as VP of engineering. A retired senior VP was hired to develop a 3-year curriculum with a dedicated talent program manager to manage this program daily. There were multiple days of intensive training every two months by invited external and internal speakers. Internal speakers were mostly from different levels of executive leaders, sharing their career experiences and introductions to their divisions or departments. During each training section, we were given practice projects to investigate, report, and present the findings and solutions. The projects usually came from ongoing and challenging hot topics of different divisions and departments of EM NP. We were provided a completion Certificate after three years of intensive training.

16.3.7 Mentor in EM NP Corporation

Each member of this leadership program was assigned a mentor from the executive leaders of EM NP. I was lucky to have Patrick Rossi, COO (Chief Operating Officer) of EM NP, as my mentor. Patrick was one of the critical people (贵人) in my career with LE and EM corporation after 2013. Despite his busy working schedule as COO, he arranged to meet me at his office every two weeks for one hour. We reviewed what I learned from the last meeting, and he patiently answered my questions regarding the company, including its history, current status, and future. Patrick had been in a senior executive position at EM for over 30 years. He was the president of the division across Europe, the Middle East, and Africa before he was promoted to COO of NP. He usually came to the office before 6:00 am and left after 8:00 pm daily. I learned a lot from him about the upstream society of the USA and how high-level corporation leadership works. It gave me the confidence and knowledge to be a leader in this multicultural and multi-ethnical society. **I appreciated his sincere guidance, support, and help a lot.** We have still been in contact each year since he retired.

16.3.8 Annual US-China Commerce Conference in a Private Jet with EM President

One day in 2014, I surprisingly received a notice from HR that I was invited to the US-China Commerce Conference and Banquet in Washington, D.C. I would be picked up by the private jet of EM's president from St. Louis in the later afternoon, together with three more colleagues from the divisions of EM in Columbus and Dayton, Ohio. Fortune 100 companies in the USA were invited to attend this conference. Bob, the president of EM NP, also sent an email to all of us attending this conference in the invitation. I drove to the Columbus International Airport before 3:00 pm and parked in a nearby side terminal dedicated to private airplanes. Three other colleagues joined me soon in a comfortable and private room before we were led to board a jet. The luxury private jet was built in France, costing more than US$60 million in 2010, dedicated to the use of EM's President. I heard later that EM had this kind of private jet fleet for its senior executives, including the Chairman, CEO, President, senior corporate executives, and the president of each business unit. The President of EM sat in the front seat, and we sat in the seats behind him.

There was a three-seat sofa and a small round conference table in the middle so a small conference meeting could be held. Those executives flew in this kind of jet across the Americas, Asia, and Europe continents. They slept over the trip on the plane to start working right after the landing. The waitress handed us a menu full of nice meals after taking off. We also met a gentleman who introduced himself as an air marshal. After the 911 event in 2001, all private planes heading to DC were required to have security guards to prevent any terrorist attack. While we were chatting, the president of EM was working on the airplane. After about one hour, we landed in DC. We were picked up by a limousine arranged by EM and headed to the conference's hotel. A big cocktail party was held about one hour before the official dinner. There were more than 100 tables in a huge conference room. Each Fortune 100 corporation occupied one table. The Chairman and CEO of EM chaired our table. He was quite talkative and asked me a brief question. Steak and chicken were served at the dinner, with salad and dessert. After the dinner, several celebrities spoke to the audience, including Dr. Henry Kissinger, a US congressman and the Chinese ambassador to the USA. The conference ended at about 10:00 pm, and we boarded the same private jet back to Columbus Airport. The private plane then headed back to St. Louis. That was the only time I boarded a private plane. Later, I learned that I was selected because of the recommendation of my mentor, Patrick.

16.3.9 Management of Engineering Teams

After joining LE/EM in 2006, I got a chance to manage several engineering teams at different times. The first one was a software development team to develop a web-based cooling performance and energy prediction tool for sale, marketing, engineering, service, and customers. The team members included computer software developers with CS (Computer Science) degrees and thermal modeling engineers with advanced mechanical engineering degrees.

There were several core team members in Columbus, Ohio. A team of developers in Slovakia was added later. I also hired two engineers in Mexico in 2019. Some signed a farewell card in October 2021 when I resigned from the company. **Their comments were a great gift to me, demonstrating that I had successfully managed a culturally diverse professional team in the past 15 years.** The following are their words in the greeting card:

"Thank you, Walter, for everything. It was a pleasure for me to work under your leadership, professionally and personally. I like you very much, so I will miss you a lot on our team. I will miss our time in restaurants during lunch and dinners we spent together tasting a lot of exotic food. So, for me, the Columbus visit will not be as before anymore. Thanks."
-From Martin Kovac

"I feel very grateful to have had the opportunity to have you as my supervisor. Thank you for your support and understanding all these years. I wish you all the best for your future endeavors."
-From Maria Admos

"Thank you for all the leadership and for being a great person and mentor."
-From Punjabi Ray

"Thank you for all of your leadership and bring our team to success."
-From Cheng Shen

"It was an honor to meet you and work with you. Thanks for all the guidelines during my first weeks in the company. All the best."
-From Santigo Gracia

"Wish you the best. Thank you for everything."

-From Samuel Sanchez

"Thank you for being such a great manager. Best of luck with your future goals."
-From Bob Smith

From 2014 to 2019, I got a chance to have another team, including mechanical design engineers, designers, and others, to develop a new product in Columbus.

I also led and coached young teams in China on advanced development projects of global microchannel heat exchangers, NPD (New Product Development) of global microchannel Condenser, CFD, and FEA teams to serve global projects.

Finding, hiring, developing, and retaining the right talents were the critical and the most challenging parts of managing a team. The skill set for most of my team's positions was unique and hard to find in the market. It took me sometimes more than six months to 12 months to find a qualified candidate. In many cases, the candidate did not have a green card or a work permit in the USA and required sponsorship from the company, which was not allowed after 2015. Another challenge of managing my team was the cultural differences among team members from different countries such as India, Sri Lanka, China, Mexico, Greece, Slovakia, and the USA. Getting them to work well together as a team was also a challenge. It could lead to official complaints or even legal lawsuits if a team member felt treated unfairly. Those senior team members with unique technical skills could easily find better jobs outside the company. It wasn't easy to satisfy them without many incentives such as promotions, bonuses, etc.

As a manager of critical teams, I also needed to work and negotiate well with my peers from marketing, service, sales, procurement, manufacturing, engineering NPD, and others on their challenging and sometimes unrealistic requirements. **Almost every month, I had to emotionally and positively answer challenging questions myself in a conference room full of people from multiple departments. I also got to defend my team's position and propose a new offering to satisfy all.**

Managing up could be challenging, too, especially with new bosses. Sometimes, I had to prepare a lot of material to educate them and convince them of the right approach. Sensitive managers might find it difficult to help me defend the position of my teams. I had to do much more to help my managers in those cases.

Sometime in 2016, I was offered a promotion opportunity to lead multiple advanced teams within EM NP in North America. The company was preparing to consolidate various R & D teams into one advanced center and needed a leader. After careful consideration, I declined the offer, which surprised the company. My mentor said I probably still did not know what I wanted to do going forward. I told the company that that position was not a real job I liked as most of my time would be spent preparing PowerPoint slides, attending many global meetings, and answering questions from senior executives. No real development work would be involved for me as this center's leader because my team's managers would do it. Another reason I declined the offer was my health situation, which I did not tell the company. As the leader of this center, I had to work seven days a week and deal with multiple disciplines, from mechanical engineering, electrical engineering, computer science, lab testing, control firmware development, and more. I had the intellectual capability, but my health conditions would not allow me to do that. **This is like you can see the peak of a big mountain and know how to get there, but your physical conditions prevent you from going forward.** I understood that was the only chance to climb up to a higher position in this global corporation. I had to choose to give it up because of poor health.

16.3.10 From EM to VE and Resignation

EM sold our division of EM NP to Plat Investment in 2016. The new corporation was called VE. A new CEO and president, Steve, was named right after the transaction. As expected, there were major organizational changes after the acquisition. Many senior executives were changed. Employee benefits were cut substantially to make more profit for the investors. Many good people, including Ryan Meyer, also chose to leave the company. I started to feel uncomfortable working in this kind of environment and wanted a change. I told families in 2018 that I might retire soon due to my health and stressful working environment. In 2019 and 2020, Dyland Martin and Brandon Wayne became my managers as Larry moved to another position. They were both nice people. In March 2020, the COVID-19 pandemic started, and we were all required to work from home. This gave me some relief from the stressful life in the office. I was able to hang on for 18 more months until October 2021, which helped my retirement finances, too. In August 2021, I informed the company that I wanted to resign, which was a big surprise to my manager, company HR, and many colleagues. I did give the company almost two months to transfer my responsibilities and find a replacement. My team in Columbus had a farewell lunch with me after working from home for almost 18 months.

I had been overworking since childhood and was exhausted physically and mentally by 2021. I needed to escape this stressful life and relieve myself to live a normal, peaceful life. Besides recovering from my poor health, I did not expect to spend a huge effort to help Patrick pull away from his failure after my resignation.

16.4 Family Life

16.4.1 Loss of Three Closest Family Members Within Three Years

My mother's health declined greatly at the end of 2011 after suffering from Alzheimer's for several years. As described in part I, she passed away in April 2012 at 84. I was lucky to see her before her last days and attended the funeral. It was during the funeral that I felt badly about the toxic environment in my hometown on money. Everything was about making money, even at funerals and weddings. Gift money, or so-called Hongbao (红包), was everywhere in pretty much every occurrence because of face problems (面子). This phenomenon was probably due to widespread capitalism and over-commercialization since 1978. Some people had lost their passion and care for unlucky, poor, and weak ones because of uncontrollable factors, especially when those persons were strangers. The day my mother passed away, her body was put in the ancestor's spiritual hall (灵堂) of our village's old building, which housed all the deceased's spirit tablets (牌位) By the tradition of our hometown, all of her children were required to stay by her body all day and night until the funeral on the 2nd day. We could hear wild cats walking and meowing on the roof that night. It was said that if family members did not always guard the body, the cat would eat it. In that case, the deceased would become alive as an evil, and those still alive might be dead. **That day was the darkest day in our family since our father died in 1968**. SiGe was fighting for his own life in Fuzhou's tumor hospital on that day because his cancer had reappeared. He was not with us to guard the dead body of Mother that night and could not attend the funeral on the 2nd day. In the afternoon of that day, ErGe got a call from the doctor's office and was confirmed to have liver cancer from an MRI exam days ago. He was then with DaGe, SanGe, and me in that spiritual hall. ErGe went directly to Fuzhou Tumor Hospital for surgery on liver cancer right after the funeral of our mother. Because of his overall poor health, no chemotherapy was performed after the surgery.

There is a saying in China that you have a home in your hometown when your parents are alive, and you become a guest over there when they are gone. On the day right after my mother passed away, SanGe showed me a few leftover items my mother had, including the picture of my graduation photo with my class in Lindun Wuqi School. I felt sad and different when entering the same room where my mother used to stay, sitting on that old king-size bed I used to sleep in and play card games with my brothers, and opening the same drawer I used to store my private items during my childhood.

SiGe continued fighting for his life with a rare abdomen cancer until April 2013, going through 13 rounds of painful and expensive chemotherapy treatments. He had the same disease as the past Venezuela president, Chavez. I went back to see him in April 2013 and stayed with him every day in the hospital for one week. Three days before he passed away, I talked to him over the phone and started to feel the weakness of his voice. **SiGe passed away at the age of 51 in Lindun after using up all of his life savings.** Many families, friends, and colleagues had provided him with financial help, including donations. It broke my heart to see SiGe leaving this world at such a young age. He didn't have enough time to enjoy the good life he deserved.

ErGe's health deteriorated at the beginning of 2015. His appetite declined at the beginning of 2015. I went back in April 2015 to see him and found he lost much weight. At the beginning of June 2015, he started to bleed a lot in the restroom and went to Changtai Hospital immediately. I called him from the USA and told him this might be the right time to leave his final words to the family. **His last**

words with me in Lindun were, "It was quite hot here."
He passed away one day later in Lindun at the age of
62. With that, I lost three of my closest family members within three years, from 2012 to 2015, which crushed me in spirit and hurt my health.

DaGe had lived a comfortable retirement life in Lindun since his early retirement at 55 in 2004. His health went south in December 2020 when he had a stroke. He was found to have liver cancer soon in the comprehensive physical exam. **Without surgery, his health deteriorated in October 2021, and he passed away in December 2021 at the age of 72.** From the last video call with him, while he was in Lindun on the final day, he barely had the strength to speak to me, and his eyes were completely yellow, even though his mind was clear. I was very sad to see him die.

16.4.2 Amelia's Education and Career

Amelia started looking for an accounting position after moving to Columbus and could not find anyone in six months, even though she had several years of working experience with an associate degree in accounting. There were too many accounting professionals from several major universities in the town, including OSU, Capital University, and Franklin University. I realized this might be the time for Amelia to return to university for a BS degree in accounting. Amelia attended Franklin University and got a BS degree in 2010. She then worked as a contractor in Cardi Health and Ash until 2012 before landing a full-time position in IA. After I resigned from LE/VE in October 2021, Amelia's job continued to provide family health insurance, which is very important for us. **The retirement benefit in the USA is not quite competitive compared with many other developed countries. Almost all companies do not provide retirement pensions now. It is very expensive to purchase your own health insurance in the USA. For seniors in the USA, federal Medicare health insurance** is unavailable until they reach 65. The full social security payment is not available until they reach 67. The average social security income was about US$1700.00 per month in 2023.

16.4.3 Sharing of Life Principles with Sophia and Patrick to Succeed

After Sophia and Patrick entered their teenage life, I wrote hundreds of email letters, texts, and WeChat messages to them to patiently guide and advise them in the right direction in their education, career, and life. The following life principles were shared with them when they were old enough to understand:

Besides hard work, good technical skills, good IQ, and EQ (personal skills), the following are also important for a person to be successful in a career and personal life:

- Choice of Career: The following should be considered in the career profession so you can support yourself and your future family:

    - Are you good at the area? Can you handle the job well without too much stress for you and your future family?

    - Is there a good job market in this area?

    - Do you like it, or can you tolerate it as a job to earn a living?

- Discipline and punctuality: Be punctual or earlier on appointments and meetings. Do what needs to be done on time no matter what happens and how much difficulty you face. Sometimes, you must be strict with yourself to stick to a plan, especially when the tasks impact others.

- Be a model for people around you, especially as a leader and a manager. The book "Seven Good Habits" details how to achieve that.

- Organizational and planning skills are important, especially to managers and leaders, as other people's activities depend on you. Your team waits for your priority and schedule setup to start their daily work. Leaders need to identify potential risks and take action ahead of time to mitigate or minimize them so that the projects and their teams can be successful.

- When there are overwhelming tasks in front of you, you need to be able to pick the top priority and urgent ones and get them done on time.

- Good communication is one of the most important skills for your success. This includes listening and understanding others well first, then responding clearly on what your thoughts, ideas, answers, and plans are. Responding on time is important, especially in the professional world. It usually needs to be on the same day or within 24 hours on important requests or questions from your managers, clients, suppliers, and internal or external customers.

- "What You Should Do" vs. "What You Want To Do": Successful people always set up their goals in their career and personal life (like good health) with a list of tasks they should do to reach their goals. They will do their best to achieve those goals no matter how hard they will be with enough determination and discipline. Most people fail because they choose " What You Want To Do " instead of " What You Should Do."

- Friends: Having the right friends around you is important to be successful. Avoid those who will drag you down. Usually, those people have bad lifestyles. Be close to friends who can move you up. Usually, they have good life habits. Good friends can help you when you need them even though you should always do your best to finish tasks yourself first. Other people's time is more valuable than yours when you need their help.

16.4.4 Sophia's Education and Career

Sophia has been a good kid and an excellent student all these years. We are proud to have this lovely daughter. She could read an interesting book by herself for a long time at age four. When she was five years old, she patiently compiled a USA country map from 51 pieces of puzzles that represented complex geometrical shapes for each state. She scored almost a perfect score on the Iowa Standard National Test in the third grade when I was teaching at SJTU. I realized then that Sophia was gifted, and I should provide the best opportunities for her to grow. That was also one of the reasons I resigned from SJTU and returned to work in the USA. When we moved to York, PA, she was confirmed by the school as a gifted student at the age of ten and was allowed to attend special classes. She published two poems that year with her English teacher's encouragement. Sophia started playing violin at age nine when I returned from SJTU to Kansas City. She became the concert Master of her high school orchestra later on. Sophia had an excellent SAT score and perfect scores on the PSAT and ACT before her college application. In 2014, she received several scholarships for her 4-year college study at OSU (Ohio State University), including the National Finalist Scholarship, the Battelle Scholarship, and the LE Scholarship. Those scholarships covered all of her 4-year tuition and the cost of living. In 2018, she was admitted to the University of Pittsburgh Medical School without a gap and got her MD degree (Medical Doctor) as an honor graduate in May of 2022. In June 2022, she started her medical residency at the University of Washington in Seattle.

The Happiest Moment to Spend for MCAT Exam and Medical School Applications

Sophia continued excelling at OSU during her undergraduate studies and had a 3.99 out of 4.0 GPA in all her classes. She started her major in Biology as a pre-med student first and changed to Neuroscience in the 2nd semester, which was closer to medical fields. However, she wanted to move to public health in her junior year after a trip to India with a couple of students from public health school. **I spent a huge effort to convince her that the job prospects of a public health student were quite limited and that she should go to medical school with her academic capabilities. She later wanted a gap year after graduation before going to medical school, probably influenced by her friends. Again, I had to persuade her to directly apply for a medical school without a gap as her background was so strong.** At the end of 2016, she finally agreed to take the MCAT exam in January 2017 so she could apply for medical school in the summer of 2017. This way, she could attend medical school in the fall of 2018 after her undergraduate graduation in May 2018. **I had been a frugal person pretty much all of my life. But it was** the happiest moment when I paid the fees for Sophia's **MCAT** exam and her medical school application because I knew she would have a bright career future going forward.

Left: White Coat Ceremony Aug 2018 at UPMC
Right: May 2022 Sophia Graduation with MD

16.4.5 Patrick's Struggle on Education and Career

Patrick's growth path has been quite different from Sophia's as a boy. He was sent back to China to live with families in Changtai for about two years when I was teaching at SJTU. Patrick had been a lovely boy before he was 12 years old. He started behaving as a typical rebellious teenager at 14 in high school, probably influenced by his peers. During that period, he often wanted to go outside of home to hang out with friends at 11:00 pm when we were ready to go to bed, even in bitterly cold seasons. Amelia and I tried very hard to push him to focus on study during his junior year of high school. With a strong resistance, Patrick did more than 30 ACT and SAT practices. I reviewed the results of every practice in detail, especially in math, to show him where to improve. Fortunately, he got good scores on the ACT and SAT and was admitted to Fisher College at OSU in 2020 with a small scholarship. When the global COVID pandemic started in 2020, remote schooling became routine, badly impacting many college students, including Patrick. He skipped many classes, missed many assignments, and fell behind on schoolwork. His GPA dropped dramatically in his sophomore and junior years. Patrick struggled with several key courses at Fisher College, including Accounting I and II, which almost forced him to drop out of school.

The worst period was from the summer to the end of 2022. In May 2022, he came home with a sling around his arm due to a dislocated shoulder that occurred when he was playing basketball. We learned on the same day that he failed again in Accounting I in the spring of 2022 and could not continue taking any classes at OSU. I quickly checked and helped him register at Columbus State University one day before the enrollment deadline so he could take the same Accounting I class there. He took just that accounting I class the whole summer and barely passed eventually. The credit was transferred to OSU. This allowed him to continue his school in the fall of 2022 with a special petition and permission from his advisor and an academic committee of Fisher College. **In the middle of fall 2022, he suddenly told me that he wanted to drop out of college because he failed miserably in the middle-term exam of the accounting II class.** Accounting II was also one of the key courses he had to pass to continue his studies in any remaining classes. In the same month, two of his best high school friends dropped out of college because they failed their schoolwork. I patiently asked him not to give up and to seek help from his advisor. He listened and re-enrolled in that accounting II class in spring 2023 and other core business classes, which were also specially approved by the academic committee with the strong support of his advisor. **During this period, I spent a huge effort understanding his situation, went into details of his curriculum, analyzed his weaknesses, taught him how to improve his studies, and encouraged him to keep trying and figuring out how to succeed.** I also provided him with rides many times to different campuses to take exams in accounting classes. Mentally, he was not resilient during this period and developed anxiety due to his life habits and repeated academic failure. There have not been enough medical providers for anxiety patients in the USA during and after the global pandemic. Some medical providers would not accept our insurance program. Most could only have practicing nurses offering remote online visits to treat the patients. **It took me many hours to call a dozen potential medical providers and eventually find one suitable MD doctor for Patrick at the end of 2022.** Luckily, he passed Accounting II in the fall of 2022 and could enroll in all remaining finance classes in the spring of 2023. By then, he had read the first several chapters of my book, which should have helped him too psychologically. In February 2023, he dislocated his shoulder again during a basketball game. I searched for and found a good orthopedic surgeon, Dr. SS, in Columbus and arranged an MRI exam on Patrick's shoulder. After reviewing the MRI exam, Dr. SS suggested that he needed major surgery, which was done on May 8, 2023. The surgery cost us a lot, even with the help of insurance coverage. **I also had to step in heavily to help Patrick as a driver and a parent, from doctor appointments to surgery and recovery care.**

Amelia and I also encouraged Patrick to apply for a summer internship at the end of 2022, which could help him build his confidence. He tried and unexpectedly got a summer intern opportunity at MC, a global Fortune 100 corporation. Patrick performed well during those 9-week internships in the summer of 2023 and was offered a full-time position starting in the summer of 2024. He did well in the remaining classes and graduated with a BS in May 2024. Amelia and I were excited and happy to attend his graduation ceremony on May 5th, 2024, on the OSU campus.

16.4.6 Family Vacations and Tourist Visits

Visit to Atlanta in 2007

We drove to Atlanta during the Christmas holidays in 2007 and stayed at the home of CZ Guo. That was the first time both families had met each other since 1997, when we moved from Tallahassee to UIUC, except for a short meeting at the Atlanta airport in 2005 with CZ. Surprisingly, two other friends' families lived in the same neighborhood as CZ's. They were JX Dong and KW. JX also studied at the University of Iowa and came to Iowa on the same plane as Amelia. KW graduated from the Department of Hydraulic Engineering in Tsinghua in 1985. We lived in the same dormitory building in Tsinghua from 1980 to 1985. Our family visited the Zoo and Stone Mountain Park in Atlanta during that trip. On the way back to Columbus, we stayed one night in Chattanooga, Tennessee, and toured the Raccoon Mountain Caverns.

Visit to Beijing and Hometown in the Summer of 2010

In the summer of 2010, we visited Beijing and Changtai Fujian for two weeks. It was the first time my own family had visited Beijing, where I attended Tsinghua University. We saw old friends and classmates, including CY Shen, WZ Yin, and WH Feng. I showed my family the dormitory building I stayed in for five years, from 1980 to 1985, while touring the Tsinghua campus. We got to taste the well-known Beijing Duck and hot pot with lamb during the trip. We also visited the Great Wall, Tiananmen Square, The Palace of Museum, the Mausoleum of Mao Zedong, The Summer Palace, Yuanmingyuan Park, the Beijing Olympic Center, the Campus of Beijing University, and the Temper of Heaven. It was also the first time I toured the Beijing University campus, even though I had lived with its neighbors for five years before.

After several days of touring in Beijing, we visited families in Changtai. That was the last time we had a complete family union in Lindun, including my mother and four older brothers.

Cruise Trip to Bahama during Christmas Break of 2010

In Christmas break of 2010, we had our first cruise vacation with several other families. It was a long trip lasting almost ten days. We first drove to Columbia in South Carolina and stayed there for two nights. On 2nd day, we drove to Charleston, South Carolina, to tour the city and an aircraft Carrier. That was the first time we saw an aircraft carrier. Charleston was well-known for the popular novel and movie "Gone with the Wind." On 3rd day, we drove to Jacksonville, Florida, to board the cruise ship in the evening. We stayed on the cruise ship touring the Bahamas island for five days. The food on the cruise ship was plenty and good. Many people were seasick on the first day on the boat. Fortunately, my family and I did not have it. We played many card games with friends, which probably was not the best activity on a cruise ship. On the way back to Columbus, we also visited Duke University and North Carolina University by staying there one more night. I did not sleep well in hotels and cruise ships during the whole trip, which was not good for my liver.

Visit to Xian and Home in the Summer of 2014

Our family visited Xian while I was on a business trip there. They got to see the Terra Cotta Warrior Museum, the downtown area of Xian, the Ming Dynasty City Wall, and the site for the Xianwumen Event, where Li Shiming (李世民) of the Tang Dynasty killed his two brothers and became the emperor eventually. Amelia was quite impressed with the food in Xian. We got to see families back in Changtai during that trip, which was not easy for me as I had just lost my mother in 2012 and SiGe in 2013.

School Visit to Eastern Coast in the Summer of 2013

Our family had school visits and vacations in the summer of 2013, as Sophia needed to apply for colleges in the fall of 2013. We drove to Boston with a one-night stay in Syracuse at midway. That was the first time my family had visited this city. Harvard and MIT were impressive, as expected. Amelia got to meet her long-time college friend, Nancy Yu. Nancy came from Xiamen and graduated from Fujian Normal University with Amelia's class. Nancy and her kids showed us the downtown area of Boston nicely. We had a good time with them that day. Our hotel was a bit far away from the downtown area. We parked our car near the subway station and toured the city by subway. Our next stop was Yale University in New Haven, Connecticut. We arrived at the booked hotel in the early evening and found it in a sketchy area. The hotel was booked online before we left Columbus, Ohio. After checking into that hotel room, I realized it was not safe to stay there. **We quickly searched, booked, and moved into another hotel in a safer area that night by wasting one night's hotel charge.** Yale's campus was classic, and we liked the university. After Yale, we drove past New York City to Princeton University. Princeton's campus was also classic, like Yale's. Both campuses were in small towns and were good for students to focus on studying. We stopped at the University of Pennsylvania campus in Philadelphia before heading to Johns Hopkins University in Baltimore. The University of Pennsylvania and Johns Hopkins were in downtown areas with less safe neighborhoods. John Hopkins was well-known for its medical school.

Visit to Zhuhai and Macao

In April 2015, I had a business trip to visit a potential supplier in Zhuhai. The 2nd day after the business visit was Saturday. I decided to tour Macao myself that day. The line to Macao from Zhuhai was long. I patiently waited for hours before entering the city. Similar to Hong Kong, this was a crowded and old city. There were many hundreds of years old buildings from Portugal period. The food was as good as the typical ones from Guangdong. More people could speak Mandarin than those in Hong Kong.

Visit to Disney in Florida during Spring Break of 2015

Kids in the USA always want to visit Disney World at least once. The vacation trip, especially the entrance tickets, was quite expensive. In the spring break of 2015, we flew directly to Orlando, Florida, stayed in a hotel, and rented a car for one week using my accumulated airline mileage. Sophia and Patrick enjoyed the trip a lot, even though one "wand" with a small sensor cost more than US$40.00 inside Harry Potter World. They were also old enough to remember the experience. I got bored with some of the parks. One day, I sent them to the park and returned to the hotel to watch some movies in the hotel room in the morning. After lunch, I found a good theater nearby and watched another popular movie before returning to pick up Amelia and the kids.

Driving Trips to Key West, Miami, Tampa, Tallahassee, and Atlanta During the Christmas Break of 2016

During our stay in Tallahassee, Florida, from 1993 to 1997, Amelia and I did not visit Miami and Key West. We embarked on a long driving trip during the Christmas of 2016 from Columbus, Ohio, to Key West, with several stops in Atlanta, Miami, Tempa, and Tallahassee. The whole trip lasted more than ten days. Sophia helped drive a lot, which relieved Amelia and me. We stopped at the home of XH He in Atlanta on the 1st night. They were our friends back in Kansas City before 2004. On the 2nd day, we drove almost 12 hours to reach the hotel in south Miami. This way, we could easily visit Key West on the 3rd day. Key West was beautiful, as expected. On the 4th day, we visited Miami Beach, its downtown, and Fort Lauderdale. On the 5th day, we drove through the big Cypress Wildlife Area on Highway 41, passed Fort Myers, and reached the hotel in Tampa. After one day's visit to Tampa, we drove to Tallahassee on the 7th day to stay at the home of CX Xu. They were our friends back in FSU. On the 8th day, we had lunch with Dean Shen and his wife, which was unexpectedly the last farewell to Dean Shen as he passed away in June 2017. On the same day, we drove to Atlanta for dinner at CL Luo's home before heading to CZ Guo's home that night. CL and his family were our friends and neighbors on the same street back in Dublin, Ohio, for several years. They moved to Atlanta in 2016 due to a job change. On the morning of the 9th day, on Christmas Eve, I found a flat tire in our car. I had to replace it with a new tire in NTB (National Tire and Battery) on the 10th day before we drove back to Columbus.

That long trip was very hard for me because I continued having dizziness and symptoms of hepatitis B without good sleep on the road.

Visit to California During Christmas Break of 2017

Amelia and Patrick had never visited California before 2017. Sophia visited San Francisco to attend a technical conference when she was working as a summer intern with an OSU professor in 2016. I have made several business trips to Los Angeles before. We flew directly to San Francisco, rented a car from the airport, and checked into the hotel by the airport. The hotel's fire alarm sounded midnight on our first day in San Francisco. We and hundreds of guests quickly moved outside the hotel for a while. As suggested by HD Huang, we took the tour bus around San Francisco's downtown area, which turned out to be a good trip. HD nicely invited us to have a good dinner at home that night. We got to see her daughter and the family of her high school friend. San Francisco was a nice city, though the housing prices were very high. After two days of visits to San Francisco, we drove to Los Angeles to check in at a hotel near the home of PH Huang. TH Huang and his family also traveled from San Diego to meet us. Los Angeles was a big metropolitan city. The traffic was bad, and it took a long time to drive from one place to another. Sophia got a chance to visit the home of her friend in OSU. We also got to see the GP Li's family. Finally, we drove back to San Franciso, stayed at a hotel for one night, returned the car on the final day, and flew back to Columbus.

Trips back to Changtai and Lindun in the Summer of 2018

Sophia had just graduated from OSU and was going to attend UPMC (University Pittsburgh Medical School) that fall. It was a happy trip for us. On the 2nd day back to Changtai, our family and families from Amelia's side, including her parents, visited Quanzhou for one day. We got a chance to board a high-speed train from Zhangzhou to Quanzhou. Quanzhou was a nice city with ancient temples from the Tang Dynasty. That night, we had a good dinner in Zhangzhou hosted by LH. LH was Amelia's cousin back in Fangyang. The following weekend, we visited the family in Lindun and had lunch in a local restaurant. I got a big fishbone stuck in my throat and was rushed to a hospital in Xiangcheng to have a doctor remove it. It would be dangerous if it were not taken out quickly. It was the last time I saw DaGe in person, as he passed away in 2021. HH Zheng came to Changtai from Xiamen to see my family during that trip. I casually informed families in Changtai that I might have to resign from my current job soon due to the health issues discussed below.

Since we moved to Columbus, we have also taken short trips to nearby towns like Cleveland, Cincinnati, Dayton, Indianapolis, and Chicago. In the Cleveland Museum, we saw Zhaoling Liujun (昭陵六 骏) of Tangtaizhong Li Shimin from 1500 years ago.

16.5 Personal Health Management

16.5.1 Reappearance of Chronic Hepatitis B

My health problems came back in 2011, during the annual physical check. I was found to have an abnormal liver function on ALT and AST. The trigging factors might be the frequent international travels on my job that I did not have good rest, plus a 10-day vacation trip to the cruise of Bahama. We drove from Columbus to Jacksonville, Florida, during that cruise trip in December of 2010. My family doctor, Dr. CF Shen, ordered more tests on my liver, including DNA virus, and found that I had active chronic Hepatitis B again with a virus level of more than one million. In 2004, I was found to have active Chronic Hepatitis B when I was teaching at SJTU. I took some antiviral medicine for several months in Shanghai then, and the liver function became normal later. Dr. Shen referred me to a specialist, Dr. Smith, for a further exam. Dr. Smith ordered a liver biopsy for me and found that I had an inflammation of my liver. He suggested I take the latest anti-virus medicine, which was very expensive in 2011. It would cost more than US$1000.00 per month then, and I needed to take it for the rest of my life. I calmly told him that I could not afford it because my job as an engineering manager in a manufacturing industry like HVAC was not stable enough to guarantee the long-term stability of income. I suggested to him that I take the Chinese medicine of Xiaoyaoyan (消遥丸) as it only cost less than US$5.00 per month at that time. DaGe had taken this medicine to treat his chronic Hepatitis B for many years. In the next several months, I started to have several typical symptoms like dark urine, loss of appetite, and tiredness. I could not sleep well at bedtime because of my hot feet, even in the freezing wintertime. Fortunately, those symptoms did not last long, and I could continue my job. My ALT and AST returned to normal several months later after I took Xiaoyaoyan and had a good rest. **I understood that I was gambling on my health, even my life, without following the advice of Dr. Smith to take an anti-virus Western medicine right away due to financial reasons.** I was asked to have an ultrasound exam on the liver every six months, DNA liver virus, and blood tests on the liver function every three months since 2011. Dr. Smith also performed endoscopy on me in 2011 and 2017 to make sure my stomach was fine because of concerns about my duodenal ulcer bleeding in 1994.

My liver DNA virus fluctuated since 2011 and started to spike up in 2016 with abnormal ALT and AST. My blood pressure went up for the first time in my life, up to 140 and 95 at that time, with a high heart rate of 90s since 1991. Dr. Smith told me it might be time that I started treating my Hepatitis B using modern anti-virus Western medicine. After a period of hesitation, I agreed in the spring of 2017 after finding that the price of anti-virus medicine had dropped significantly by more than ten times. That medicine was just over the patent protection period. The generic version was available at about US$50.00 per month in 2017. Fortunately, that medicine worked well with me. My ALT, AST, and DNA virus levels went normal quickly within two months, preventing further liver damage. DNA virus went down further to an undetectable level after one year of treatment. In the spring of 2021, Dr. Smith retired. He recommended another gastroenterologist, Dr. Anne Bedi, to me in the same group before his retirement.

16.5.2 Vertigo

One afternoon in the spring of 2013, I was in my office and suddenly had a strong dizziness sitting on my chair. The whole building and roof were spinning quickly. I was nauseous and wanted to vomit. It lasted for less than 30 seconds. At midnight of that day, I felt again in the bed that the whole room and roof were spinning, and I could barely walk over to the bathroom to vomit. In the early morning of the 2nd day, Amelia accompanied me to the emergency room at Riverside Hospital of Columbus. After more than four hours of examination, including a CT of the brain, I was told that I had Vertigo for unknown reasons. **Vertigo was the most painful disease and had the most difficult symptoms I have ever experienced in my whole life. It was like the end of the world for me. Some Vertigo patients described that it was worse than death (生不如死)** It is still one of the most difficult diseases to diagnose the root cause in the medical field. There were too many possible reasons for Vertigo from an online book compiled by a Vertigo patient, including brain diseases, heart diseases, neck issues, diabetes, lack of sleep, stress, anxiety, ear stones, etc. I pretty much exhausted all exams with visits to different kinds of physicians, including ENT after that, and could not identify the reason for my Vertigo. In the fall of 2020, I experienced Vertigo again and felt very bad. Dr. Wright from the Columbus ENT group examined the issue carefully and did not find an obvious root cause. He suggested that I do therapy online based on Dr. Michael Teixido's YouTube video on BPPV (Benign Paroxysmal Positional Vertigo or Ear Stone). The treatment was painful but helpful, as it was like going through another round of Vertigo. I would sweat so much that my whole clothes went wet after the therapy. After several days of treatment, my symptoms disappeared. It was the period that I told myself it might be the right time for me to quit my job and rest well to improve my overall health, which led to my resignation in October 2021.

16.5.3 Kidney Stone and Blood in Urine

My kidney stone re-appeared in 2011 during an annual visit to the Urologist, Dr. Pak. There was invisible blood in my urine sample. A CT exam found that I had small kidney stones of around 2 to 3 mm. I also had a bladder cystoscopy that year by Dr. Pak and found that my bladder was fine. He wanted me to have a close check every year on my urine system before doing anything. In 2019, a regular ultrasound exam on my liver and kidney showed something in my kidney. Dr. Pak ordered a CT exam and found there were 3 to 4 mm kidney stones in both of my kidneys. During the annual physical check of 2021, the invisible urine blood was found again. Dr. Pak performed a cystoscopy on my bladder. Everything with my bladder was fine. He believed the urine blood should be from those kidney stones. I frequently feel pains in my right upper abdomen area in the last 15 years, probably due to the existence of kidney stones. I was told to check closely every year and let Doctor Pak know whenever there were severe symptoms.

16.5.4 Sleep Apnea

I sent the following message to Dr. ZX Yang, a neurologist referred by my family doctor, Dr. Shen, on February 13, 2018. **It showed how bad my physical health was in 2018. Considering my family history of health and the recent passing away of SiGe and ErGe at young ages, I quietly prepared a brief written will to store in the security box of the bank. At the same time, I casually shared the key information of family financial accounts with Amelia.** Doctor Yang was very experienced. After reviewing the CT on the brain ordered by Dr. CF Shen, he ordered an Echocardiogram of my heart first, which confirmed my heart was fine. He then suspected that I had Sleep Apnea and referred me to Dr. Johnson, a pulmonologist at OhioHealth. After several rounds of testing and exams, it was found that I had moderate to severe Apnea with AHI (Apnea-hypopnea index) up to 28. Dr. Johnson decided that I needed to wear a CPAP machine during sleep. My health, especially dizziness and blood pressure, improved greatly after several months of wearing a CPAP machine at night. The AHI index fell to below five quickly with the CPAP machine. The blood pressure became normal in the fall of 2018.

"Hi, Dr. Yang:

Since my last visit to you, my dizziness has not improved or is getting worse to some extent, as below:

- I had difficulty walking most days and most of the time. It felt like the floor was moving or I was stepping on cotton. It was worse when walking on a hard floor or shining floor.
- I felt more dizzy when looking at rotating pictures on a computer, watching TV, or sitting on a rotating chair.
- I could suddenly feel dizzy sometimes, even when I am sitting
- I could feel dizzy right after lying in bed for a short time.
- On the evening of February 12, a strong tightness in my leg occurred after exercise, dinner, and shower, which made it harder for me to walk. It got better after robbing the leg and doing some leg exercises. After all the checking I have done in the last several years, including a cardiac diagram on the heart, CT on the brain, and ENT checking on the ear, are there other reasons like the following?
- Is the neck bone pushing the nerve? I have recently experienced numbness in my backbone when bending to eat or brush my teeth.
- Low blood supply to brain and feet?

I have had foot pain for several years and have handled it with therapy.

Thank you. Walter Lin"

16.5.5 Other Health Issues

Eye Surgery

I had eye surgery in March 2018 to remove a caruncular nevus in my left eye, performed by Dr. Wilson. He is a good optometrist in the Ohio ENT group. This caruncular nevus had been there for a long time, probably from my young age as a boy. The doctor suggested removing it in case it might go bad. It was the first time I had a major surgery other than Colonoscopy and Endoscopy. Amelia and I arrived at Columbus Riverside Methodist Hospital by 6:00 am. The surgery started at 7:00 am. When I was pushed into the surgery room, there were six people in the operation room, including Dr. Wilson, an anesthesiologist, and nurses. I quickly went to sleep due to anesthesia and woke up probably after 9:30 am. The surgery went well, and we came home after 11:00 am. During the exam by Dr. Wilson, I also found that my eye pressure was at the border of high normal, which is a risk for glaucoma. Dr. Wilson asked me to check my eye pressure regularly.

Hernia Surgery

I found two bumps on both sides of my groin area during a shower in September 2022. They were the size of small eggs, which made me very nervous. I made an appointment to see my family doctor, Dr. Jackson, on the 3rd day. My previous family doctor, Dr. CF Shen, retired in May 2021. Dr. Jackson became my new family physician. I did not know anything about Hernias then. Dr. Jackson was experienced and told me it was a hernia that needed to be repaired by surgery. He quickly referred me to a good surgeon, Dr. Moore. The surgery was scheduled for December 2022. I also visited Dr. Pak to confirm this was a Hernia before the surgery, as the area is close to the prostate. The surgery went well, as expected. We arrived by about 6:00 am. The surgery started at 7:00 am and finished by 8:00 am. I left the surgery center after 10:00 am. The recovery process, including diet after Hernia surgery, was more complicated than eye surgery in 2018. There was constant sharp pain around the incision area for almost three days after the surgery. I refrained from using the strong pain medicine prescribed by the surgeon. Instead, I only used Advil and Tylenol. By following the requirements and procedures closely from Dr. Moore, I recovered well. I was asked to avoid heavy lifting going forward to prevent the re-appearance of the hernia and hurting the surgical incision area.

Challenging COVID-19 Pandemic Period-Both Amelia and I Got Sick in The Same Week

Sophia and Patrick got COVID-19 by the end of 2021, confirmed by tests with typical symptoms of high fever, cold, cough, and fatigue. I got very sick with symptoms similar to theirs after they came home for holiday visits. I was so cold that I trembled a lot, even in bed with all possible comforters. The house temperature was set very high on heating. Fortunately, I recovered after five days of resting in bed. This COVID-19 virus was strong even though we all had two vaccines shot before.

Amelia got her first COVID-19 at the beginning of September 2023, probably from the office. It was also the first time since 1991 that Amelia got sick with a fever lasting more than four days. I did not isolate myself well because I thought I already had COVID-19 before and also had four doses of COVID-19 vaccines. Three days after Amelia got sick, I started having a high fever. It was the first time that both Amelia and I were ill at the same time, which was very painful. Amelia was given Paxlovid for five days, which helped the fever and sore throat. I took Molnupiravir for five days, which was also helpful. After four days of fever, I started having a bad cold with a severe dry cough, sore throat, and chest congestion for another eight days. The positive side was that Amelia had better immunity against COVID-19 now.

Fast Heart Rate and Anxiety

I have been taking Atenolol since 2000 on a fast heart rate and anxiety. **My heart rate was above 90's from 1992 to 2021 for almost 30 years.** In July 2022, my heart rate dropped to around 80 after ten months of relaxation without working. At the end of 2023, my heart rate sometimes decreased to below 80 if I slept well. Dr. Jackson thought I might not need Atenolol if I continued having a relaxed life.

Allergy

I have had strong allergies since 1998, with symptoms of daily sneezing, eye itching, and nose and throat itching, similar to a cold. I used eye drops and nose spray almost daily since then. In 2004, I had a comprehensive exam, including needle testing. The doctor put more than 60 small needles on my arms to see what kind of substances were leading to my allergy. Pollen from flowers, dust, and mold were the ones I needed to avoid. My frequent sneezing might be one of the reasons leading to my hernia, as it increased my stomach pressure. Prescribed eyedrops could cost over US$200.00 on a five ml bottle, which insurance would not cover. Therefore, I tried all lower-cost counter eyedrops and stayed with brands of Opcon-A from BAUSCH LOMB, Naphcon A, Refresh Tears, and Nasal Spray of premium saline for many years. A 15 ml Opcon-A costs less than US$6.00. Sometimes, I have to take allergy medicine like Claritin during the spring and fall seasons. My allergy improved greatly by the end of 2023.

Due to allergies, I coughed a lot in the spring and fall seasons. **One morning in the spring of 2015, I coughed out blood. I quickly went to see my family doctor and**

had a blood test for TB (Tuberculosis). The results came back positive, which scared me a lot. My father died of TB. My 2nd oldest brother, ErGe, damaged his liver further during the treatment of TB in 2010 because the medicine to treat TB had severe side effects on the liver. I quickly saw Dr. Smith and Dr. Cho, an infectious disease specialist. Dr. Smith suggested that I needed to monitor my liver function each month if I had to take medicine to treat TB. Dr. Cho ordered a 2nd blood test and found a negative result. One month later, I had a 3rd blood test and was confirmed to be negative for TB, which was a great relief to me. I was fighting with Hepatitis B, Vertigo, and Sleep Apnea during that period.

16.5.6 Strict Lifestyle and Psychological Adjustment

I started to exercise regularly, like jogging and fast walking, in 1995 after almost losing my life over severe duodenal bleeding. However, I still ate salty and oily food a lot until 2011, when my Hepatitis B re-appeared. Doctors told me to eat less fat, less salty, and high-protein food. In 2015, I subscribed to Charming China TV program and got to watch several good health programs like "YanShengTan 养生堂" and "DaYiSheng 大医生" from Beijing TV and "JiankangZhiDu 健康之路" from CCTV. I watched those programs almost daily and became much more knowledgeable on medical issues and how to care for personal health. Amelia and I have had strict healthy food and lifestyle ever since. We tried to eat a variety of food full of protein, fiber, vitamins, and carbs each day. I spent more than 60 minutes doing all kinds of exercise and physical therapies like Shaolin Baduangjin (少林八段锦). Amelia and I also develop a habit of sleeping and getting up early. We usually go to bed before 11:00 pm and get up before 7:00 am. There is a saying in Chinese that you become a good doctor after experiencing long-term diseases, which applies well to me personally (久病成良医).

It was very stressful for me from May 2022 to the end of 2023 because

a) Patrick's struggle with his education and health. **I got very nervous every semester at the end of final exams before we knew his grades. I was afraid Patrick would fail again and not be allowed to take the remaining classes at Fisher College.**

b) My surgery for the Hernia and hacking of a personal computer in September 2022.

c) I discovered in early 2022 that our social security income will drop 22% in 2035, which changed my financial plan before October 2021.

d) Inflation went up more than 9% nationally in 2022

e) I lost much money in my retirement savings due to a significant bond and S&P 500 stock market drop in 2022. I had no job or pension income after my resignation in October 2021. Fortunately, most losses were recovered because the market bounced back by the end of 2023. A lot has been learned from the financial loss in 2022 on the relations among interest rates, bond return, index stock performance, global politics, the noise of Wall Street, and the media. This would help me in future retirement fund management.

Therefore, I set up the following life priorities and the principles of life to remind and guide me constantly during those difficult times. **I had many sleepless nights wondering how to pull Patrick away from falling over a steep cliff. Writing this book was part of an effort to wake him up, move away from those bad lifestyles, and be successful in his education and future career.**

Priorities of Life

1. Personal health and safety
2. Family's health and safety
3. Family happiness and harmony
4. Kid's education and career
5. Amelia's job and family health insurance
6. Retirement saving, economic status, and wealth management

Principle of Life

- **Positive**

   Stay optimistic no matter what happens. Just try your best to improve. Sometimes, you have to accept whatever will go by nature.

- **Loving**

   Love and be passionate with people around you, including family, relatives, and friends, even those you do not know well.

- **Forgiving**

   Forgive people for their past mistakes and move on to a new chapter

- **Appreciative**

   Appreciate whatever you have now, like good health, a nice family, and sufficient economic conditions for a basic life. Appreciate any help you have received from anyone when you struggled, from Lindun as a poor boy to a mature adult in Columbus now.

- **Simplifying**

> Simplifying lifestyle after retirement. Live a simple life as long as it meets basic needs. Imagine what you went through in Lindun as a boy.

- **Calm**

> Calm down in whatever situation. Do not get excited, and maintain a peaceful mind. Life journey is not always a joy. Suffering and hardship are part of what everyone endures from birth.

16.6 Hacking of Personal Computers and Protection of Personal Identity

My laptop was hacked on September 14, 2022, because I accidentally hit the wrong link. I was nervously searching for information on bumps in my groin areas before Dr. Jackson told me it was Hernia on September 15, 2022. All of our personal and financial information was stored on this computer. The following were done quickly:

(1) I changed key passwords on key accounts like banks and this laptop. I also shut down the computer within one hour after the accident.

(2) I called all credit card companies that day to change credit cards and asked them to issue alerts.

(3) I went to my bank on the 2nd day to change account numbers and checkbooks.

(4) I used my phone to change user names and passwords on the 2nd day for all financial and personal accounts.

(5) I contacted three major credit companies to issue an alert first and then locked credit reports for Amelia and me. The USA is a credit-based society. Good credit is required for most life activities, including employment, loans, renting, bank and other financial accounts, et al.

(6) I contacted all financial companies to inform them of the hacking and asked them to put more security checks and restrictions on any future transactions

(7) I brought this laptop and another old computer to Microcenter where we purchased them. I learned online that resetting the laptop to factory status can remove all potential virus software and clean the PC. With some hints from Microcenter, I reset both new and old PCs successfully for the first time at home and reinstalled the Windows system and other software myself. To be safe, I also purchased and installed antivirus software on both computers. That was one of the most stressful weeks of my life.

16.7 Trips back to Lindun and Visit to Father's Grave in October 2023

In October 2023, Amelia and I embarked on an important trip back to Changtai. **It was stressful and expensive to prepare for this trip with a visa, COVID test, health code required by customs, gifts, gift cash, and booking of air tickets and hotels in Hong Kong after multiple years of the global pandemic.** When we arrived at Hong Kong airport on the evening of Oct 8, a big typhoon shut down almost all transportation in Hong Kong. More than twenty thousand passengers were stuck in the airport and could not leave. Like many passengers, we were forced to stay overnight at the airport as we could not find any transportation to a reserved hotel, which was only one mile from the airport. **As experienced many years ago, we were disappointed that many Hong Kong locals could not speak English or Mandarin Chinese.**

They could only speak Cantonese dialect in this busy international and Chinese city. My heart rate stayed in the 90s during the whole trip until two weeks after we returned to Columbus, probably due to jet lag and stress on the trip.

Left: Lindun Families (Oct 2023)
Right: Nanjing Tulou Oct 2023 with Family of SanGe

We were emotional to see families after more than five years of separation. Amelia's father had a major surgery in March 2023 and recovered well. My oldest brother passed away in 2021. Our family added another widow. As we got older, there were more kids in the families. During the trip, the son of SanGe took us to tour Nanjing Tulou, which was about a two-hour drive from Changtai. Amelia's nephew drove us to visit the old city of Zhangzhou City.

I saw some high school classmates, including MS Shen, HL Liu, GZ Xie, GB Zhang, JB Lin, SY Dai, SY Xue, et al. I had not seen some of them since 1980. MS and his wife traveled from Fuzhou to meet us in Changtai. I had been excited to see them since 1990 when Amelia and I visited them in Fuzhou. We met HP Zhuang in front of his small grocery store on the road to MS's old residence. HP was also one of our high school classmates. He could recognize me even though we had not seen each other for over 43 years.

Status of Lindun

Starting in 2019, Lindun became a deserted town with a population of less than 10,000. Most young people went out of town to work in cities. Whoever had the capabilities moved their families to cities so their kids could have better education. Elders and young children from poor families remained, similar to most rural areas in China. Most farming lands were deserted as those elders were losing the capability to do the farming work. Few remaining young people were not interested and did not know how to do farming as the annual output was too low. Fruit like grapefruit, lychee, and longan (桂园) in the nearby mountain hills were not harvested because the market value of those fruits was lower than the cost to pick, ship, and sell. It was dark and dead silence after the evening fell. Most people would not dare to go out at night. Lindun prospered from 1995 to 2019 due to this town's booming marble stone industry. Over 500 family-owned factories were in the town during that period to manufacture raw marble stone products to be sold nationwide. The population soared to over 30,000 at that time. More than half of them were immigrant workers from other provinces like Guizhou. Less than 10% of families in Lindun became rich. Many of them drove luxury cars like BMWs and Mercedes and lived in mansions bigger than most single houses in the USA. However, those factories severely polluted the environment, including the rivers and farming lands. They also hurt the health of workers. The government shut down all of them in 2019, leading to a population decline. Many shops, restaurants and daycares were closed. The majority of the remaining people in Lindun became very poor again. **The social security income for senior peasants, like most of my childhood friends and wives of my deceased brothers DaGe and ErGe, was only about US$20.00 per month in Lindun.** Most had to work one way or another to make a basic living, even in their 70s. **They had a lousy health care program**

and couldn't afford to become sick with any major disease. I had to constantly persuade my brother SanGe to get a comprehensive physical exam because the expense was not covered by health insurance without hospitalization. Some of the peasants chose to stop treatment once they were found to have a fatal disease. Two of my neighbors in their 50s went home directly from the Changtai District Hospital without any required treatment after the doctor told them that they were found to have major diseases. They died soon at home. One of my childhood friends in his 60s was still doing labor work 12 hours per day in a small factory in a nearby town. He needed to earn money to help two unmarried sons in their 30s. There were many unmarried old male singles in Lindun, including sons of several childhood friends of mine. Some singles even had college degrees and worked in the cities of Xiamen, Zhangzhou, and Changtai District townships. No girl wanted to marry them because their families could not afford an apartment in those cities. The house prices skyrocketed in most cities of China from 2000 to 2020. The apartment price per square meter in Changtai District town was higher than in Columbus, Ohio, in 2023. The average housing price in Xiamen was more than in Seattle and Los Angeles per square meter. The average GDP and salary income per person in China was less than 20% of the numbers in the USA in 2023. At the same time, there were many ghost houses and apartment buildings in many cities due to overbuilding for the current population. A few old singles in Lindun found wives from Vietnam and Cambodia directly. There are more than 10 million college graduates each year recently in China. Almost half of them could not find a suitable job. Most of those new graduates would stay at home, including some in Lindun. Those youth did not want to take up farming or blue-collar jobs at a low income, even though they could not find decent jobs with satisfactory salaries.

I also visited the old house on deserted Lindun downtown street, which used to be a pharmacy store for my family. A photo in front of the Lindun Clinic reminded me a lot of my childhood life. **The almost collapsed house where I was born and grew up gave me many memories of a poor and warm life with my family.**

Left: Lindun Clinic
Right: Collapsed Family Pharmacy Shop Building

Childhood Bedrooms   Collapsed Childhood Kitchen

Grave of Father Water Channel River

Visit to Father's Grave

I paid a special visit to my father's grave over the nearby mountain during the trip, although it was against the religious tradition in my hometown on timing. **An innocent boy in 1968 had become a senior full of grey hair after 55 years of challenging and exciting exploration of life outside Lindun. I just wanted to let Father know I have missed him all these years and wanted to share my life experience and stories with him if possible.**

Front of Father's Grave

Brief Resume –
Walter Lin, Ph.D.

Major Life Experiences

- Childhood before School in Lindun of Changtai District, Zhangzhou City, Fujian, China (1965-1971)

- Elementary and Middle School in Lindun of Changtai District, Zhangzhou City, Fujian, China (1971-1978)

- High School, Changtai No. 1 High School, District Township, Changtai District, Zhangzhou City, Fujian, China (1978-1980)

- **Undergraduate Study, Tsinghua University, Thermal Engineering, Beijing, China (1980-1985)**

- Graduate Study, Shanghai Jiaotong University and MA Institute of China, Ocean and Naval Architecture Engineering, Shanghai, China (1985-1988)

- Research and Design Engineer, MA Institute of China, Shanghai, China (1988-1992)

- **Ph.D. Study, Dept. of Mechanical Engineering, Thermal Science, Florida State University (FSU), Tallahassee, Florida and The University of Iowa, Iowa City, Iowa, USA (1992-1997)**

- **Postdoctoral Research Associate, National Center for Supercomputing Applications (NCSA), University of Illinois at Urbana-**

Champaign (UIUC), Illinois, USA (1997-1998)

- Senior Engineer, EV and EM Corporation, Kansas City, Kansas, USA (1998-2001)

- Senior Engineer and Manager, SP Corporation, Kansas City, Kansas, USA (2001-2003)

- **Professor, School of Mechanical Engineering, Shanghai Jiaotong University, Shanghai, China (2003-2004)**

- Senior Principal Engineer, YO and JC Corporation, York, Pennsylvania, USA (2005-2006)

- **Senior Manager Product Development and Senior Development Scientist, LE, EM and VE Corporation, Columbus, Ohio, USA (2006-2021)**

- Writer, Columbus, Ohio, USA (2022 – Present)

Patents and Peer-Reviewed Technical Publications (Lead and Co-Author)

Six awarded US invention patents, a peer-reviewed technical book by Taylor & Francis Publisher and numerous peer-reviewed technical papers in the International Journals of Heat Transfer (ASME), International Journals of Fluids Engineering (ASME), International Journals of Engineering Mechanics (ASCE), International Journal of Heat & Mass Transfer, International Journals of Numerical Heat Transfer (Part A & B), International Journal of Atmospheres and Oceans, ASME TURBO EXPO, Proceeding of ASME heat transfer/fluids engineering and others.